PROVENCE

PROVENCE

Texts
Jean-Max Tixier

Translation
Peter Mc Cavana

EDITIONS EUROPÉENNES
DE MARSEILLE-PROVENCE

CONTENTS

Previous pages:
Valensole Plateau.
A fragrant purple river of lavender flows
as far as the eye can see.

Contents pages:
Camargue. Sunset on the lagoon.

INTRODUCTION

When God had completed the Creation, he realized that he had not made use of all the riches at his disposal. Therefore he decided to gather them together in a special place, a sort of heaven on earth. It was thus that he created Provence. So the legend says. And reality this to be true - particularly as there is not just one Provence, but many of them, defined by uncertain boundaries that fluctuate with the times, and all equally attractive. For the sake of simplicity, let us say that Provence is the area between the River Rhône in the West, the Var region in the East, the Mediterranean in the South, and Montélimar in the North. This is the Provence that is explored in this book.

With just a quick browse through these pages, you will realize that, paradoxically, Provence is a united entity composed of many facets. Throughout the centuries, it has gradually forged a single identity despite its internal diversity. You just have to climb over a hill, go to the next village or cross a river to find a different landscape, different customs or a different mentality. Provence is a land of contrasts, from the lagoons and marshes of the Camargue to the stony plain of La Crau, from the lofty citadel of Les Baux to the rich land of the Comtat Venaissin, from the vineyards of the Var to the olive-groves of Nyons, and from *the calanques* of Cassis to the austere Plateau of Valensole. Some parts have a certain flavor of Africa, while others are influenced by the severity of the Alps. Avignon shows Spanish influence, while Avignon, the city of the Popes, has an Italian dimension. With its particularly rich and eventful history, Provence still bears the marks of all the peoples that shaped it, including the Celts, Greeks, Romans, Barbarians and Saracens. It provides a sort of résumé of history that everyone interprets as they wish. Hospitality is written in its soil and in its past. It is also a part of tradition: in former times, when a family sat down to dinner, there was always an extra plate for any unexpected guest, for whom they set aside the "poor man's portion".

Nowadays, this hospitality is evident in many other aspects related to the general conditions of our times. Natural assets have been developed and exploited, generally without undermining their authenticity. Amenities for tourists are certainly among the best, and have not spoiled the environment. Naturally, one does not find the same facilities or attractions in the upper Verdon valley as in the Alpilles Hills, Saint Tropez or the inland areas of the Var, and one has to be thankful for this. There is something for everyone: countryside, mountains, family beaches or sophisticated beaches, and sporting holidays or holidays where you can learn about the region's culture and heritage. This is why Provence rivals with the French Riviera as the region that has the most visitors and the most holiday homes.

In addition to the beauty spots, the ancient remains, and the historic and artistic legacy, there is also the gastronomic splendor. For Provence has a lifestyle and a cuisine of its own. Everyone knows the great classics: *bouillabaisse, bourride, aïoli, soupe de poisson, soupe au pistou,* the nougats of Montélimar and Seau, the crystallized fruit of Apt and the *calissons* of Aix. But there are more local specialities, such as *poutargue* (spiced mullet roe caviar), *panisses* (chickpea pancakes), *tapenade* (olive paste), *caillette* (a sort of "paté sausage") and *olives cassées* (crushed olives), to name but a few. Adventurous gourmets will be delighted to discover them.

It is not by chance that Provence has always attracted artists: painters, from Van Gogh to Picasso, writers such as Cocteau, musicians, and actors such as Gérard Philippe, who is buried in Ramatuelle. Their genius has enhanced the region. One can visit Provence through the eyes and the sensibility of those who have portrayed it and sung its praises. It is an open-air museum, but also a living one that welcomes every visitor as a friend. And it is a land of famous festivals - crowds flock to Aix for classical music and opera, Orange for choral music, La Roque d'Anthéron for piano music, and Antibes for jazz. But let us not forget the countless lesser-known festivals that celebrate the arts in summer, when the whole of Provence wishes you all a warm welcome in a festive mood. ❧

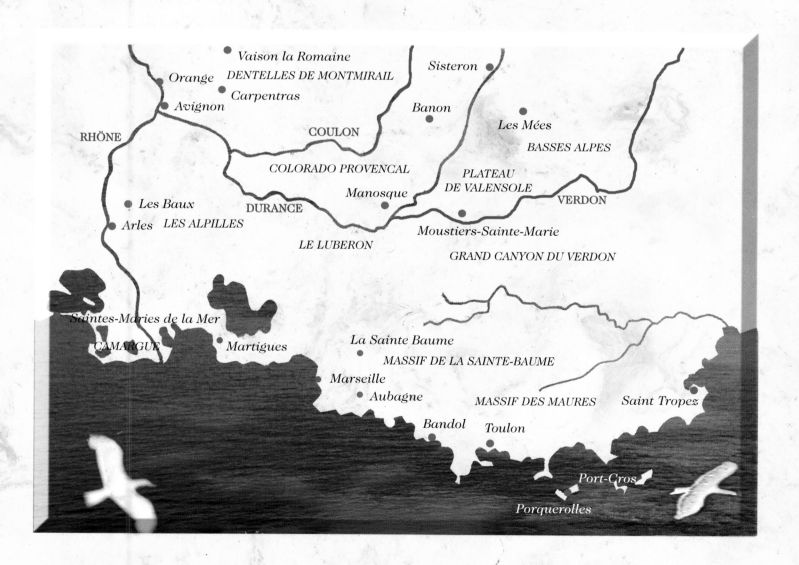

THE LANDSCAPES AND
COUNTRYSIDE OF PROVENCE

Cattle grazing on the manade (Camargue ranch).

THE CAMARGUE

Previous pages:
The colors of Provence.

Gardian at work.

The Camargue is a wild country steeped in legend that has inspired many artists. This wilderness of sand, water, salt, red behen, marsh-samphire and bullrushes is the realm of horsemen and nomads, and has an almost fantastical quality. The Camargue was formed by the delta of the River Rhône, whose branches mark the area's boundaries. Over time, this vast desolate area has gradually been created by the constant opposition and combination of the elements, shaping an unusual landscape that is unique in France. The Camargue has been described as "an island surrounded by land" and, although most of it lies in Provence, the "Little Camargue"

on the right bank of the river is actually part of the Languedoc region.

Despite a few attempts at farming, such as market gardening and particularly rice growing - developed at the cost of many disputes with cattle farmers, worthy of the best American Westerns - the Camargue is mainly used to raise animals and remains strongly influenced by the tradition of nacioun gardiano, or cattle breeding. The local people have grown accustomed to living in close contact with untamed nature and breed herds of cattle and horses. The herds of black bulls, with their lyre-shaped horns, are used for bull racing and the white horses, of the world's oldest known breed, live in the open in the *sansouire* marshland, a salt steppe scattered with unfriendly bushes that is often flooded.

Wild landscape: A channel among the reeds.

The *gardians* (Camargue cowboys), whatever their origin, form a genuine aristocracy. The traditional home is a farmhouse or the strange "cowboy hut" built with its back to the prevailing wind, with whitewashed walls and cane roofing.

While the north is mainly marshland, the south is the land of the lagoons. The largest lagoon is Vaccarès, home to the pink flamingos and also a reserve for a variety of plants and animals. The regional nature reserve is in Vaccarès. Here plant life is to be seen only rarely with salt crystals shining between the odd clump of marsh-samphire. The only living presence is that of the radiant sun that creates fleeting mirages. The marshland has, however, been drained and arid land can now be irrigated. In 1869 a network of embankments, adding to the picturesque qualities of the area, was built in an effort to tame the unpredictable Rhône river. The Camargue is therefore the result of a continual battle between river and sea,

A flock of pink flamingos in Ginès Lagoon.

Camargue ponies, tranquil monarchs of their realm.

sand and silt and of the ingenuity of the men and women who knew how to use its natural resources to their best advantage without affecting the area's wild beauty.

The town of Saintes-Marie-de-la-Mer, the capital of the Camargue, lies in the extreme south. It was so named because it was here that the saints Martha, Mary Salomé, Mary the mother of James, and their black servant, Sarah, are said to have landed in a boat. Saintes-Marie-de-la-Mer is the cradle of Provençal Christianity and is the destination for one of the region's best-attended pilgrimages. The fortified church, where the saints' relics are preserved, attracts huge crowds of worshippers twice a year, in May and October. It is a popular place with gypsies who come here to pay homage to their patron saint. ❧

A calanque nestling snugly in the white rocks - a yachting paradise.

THE CALANQUES

by Philippe Hiély

Between Marseille and Cassis, nature has shaped idyllic scenery formed about 10,0000 B.C. by a rise in sea level of at least 70 metres that submerged the estuaries of the little coastal streams, forming rocky coves known as "calanques", which are rias (narrow, drowned valleys). The hard dolomitic limestone dating from the Urgonian era was eroded by the offshore winds, creating a rugged rocky landscape with dramatic cliffs. Nothing is left of their former cover of evergreen oak, but the calanques are still beautiful. The jagged white rocks stand out starkly against the

Order, calm and serenity.

A little piece of heaven. Sugiton Calanque.

blue sea and sky in a marvellous symphony of color. As the day progresses, the acid-tones of the morning gradually change to the orange hues of the evening in a magical dance.

There are many facets to the calanques. Inhabited since prehistoric times, the Cosquer Cave contains 20,000 year old engravings and wall paintings, whereas the Lascaux caves are only 13,000 years old. The Veyre spring existed when Gyptis gave the cup to Protis 2,600 years ago, marking the foundation of Marseille.

For a long time, the coast was a haunt of local pirates or pirates from the Barbary Coast, and they probably used the Escu reservoir to replenish their stocks of water

Calanque of Rafrège-Cuou.

after a sun-scorched voyage had parched the throats of their galley slaves.

Ruined look-out posts and fortifications are reminders of the calanques' strategic importance: some of them have a bloody history. In 1805, Boucher de Perthes, who was barely 16 years old, went into the Roland Cave to look for fossils of shellfish. He was already convinced that men had lived in it thousands of years ago and, on that day, he created the science of palaeontology when he collected the first ever fossils in the history of mankind.

"Home is the fisherman"
Morgiou Calanque..

Louis XIII fished tuna in Morgiou with a silver-gilt trident. In 1720, the "Grand Saint Antoine" was placed in quarantine near Jarre Island and its cargo was secretly unloaded at Plan de Cailles, bringing the plague to Marseille and the surrounding area.

The local wildlife features a lizard whose origins can be traced back to prehistoric times. The islands were the departure point for the spread of the herring gull (Larus cachinans) that now proliferates exponentially. There are also some Bonelli eagles, some peregrine falcons whose species established Riou's reputation, and many cormorants. Botanists can study 600 species in the calanques, including the extremely rare arborescent Euphorbia and Gouffé grass, which is virtually specific to the area.

Opposite:
The luscious beauty of nature.

The calanques are a paradise for mountaineers and rock climbers - the vertical rock faces can be climbed in all seasons. They also have mystery. The underground Cassis river, once lauded by Rimbaud, pours into the calanque of Port-Miou. Its western branch ends in a submerged well that has only been explored to a depth of 145 metres. Discovering the calanques is a long dialogue with nature and with oneself.

A typical landscape in the Alpilles Hills.

THE ALPILLES HILLS AND BAUX DE PROVENCE

The jagged blue rocks of the Alpilles Hills are an extension of the Luberon Mountains. They are part of "Sacred Triangle" so dear to the folklorist Marie Mauron. Between Salon in the East and Tarascon in the West, several picturesque villages nestle among the cypress and olive trees: Le Paradou, Maussane, Mouriès, Fontvieille (with its windmill made famous by the writer Daudet in "Letters from my Mill"), Aureille, Eyguières, Eygalières and, further to the North, St Rémy with its rich collections of ancient treasures from Glanum, Graveson and Maillane. This is the very heart of Provence, the Provence of the poet Mistral. Jumbled blocks of white limestone are stacked one upon the other to create rugged cliffs and windswept

Les Baux fortress stands out in the chaos of jagged rocks shaped by the centuries.

*Lofty ruins bear witness
to a glorious past.*

eagles' nests. In these hills, where the summits are no higher than 500 metres, erosion has sculpted out stone monsters and giants. This is the land of mythical beasts, Tarasques and dragons that terrorized the local people, and the famous Golden Goat, guardian of a treasure which is no doubt more mythical than real. A land of shepherds, who are still considered a little as sorcerers, and the birthplace of prophets such as Nostradamus, the Alpilles Hills are dotted with caves and hollows such as the den of the witch Taven, where Mistral's heroine Mireille sought refuge with the injured Vincent.

Towering above this majestic landscape, the proud silhouette of the citadel of Les Baux juts into the skyline. The ruins of its castle are still haunted by the lords who dwelt there - "race d'aiglons, jamais vassale" ['a race of eaglets that were never vassals'] - the first of the great Provençal families,

The bastion of a "race of eaglets" stands proudly on top of the cliff.

descendants of Balthazar, one of the three "Wise Kings". Val d'Enfer ("The Vale of Hell") forms a natural rampart around this legendary town that has been taken over by the "merchants in the temple" and has become a top tourist attraction. This rocky spur, 800 metres long by 20 metres wide, occupies the top of the cliff. The main street climbs its way amid old Renaissance residences, many of them restored and used as shops. The visitor can admire the Eyguières Gate, the Church of Saint Vincent, the Chapel of the Pénitents Blancs (White Penitents), and the Manville Mansion. At the top end of the town, a monument to the Occitan poet Charloun Riou stands on a viewpoint from where there is a splendid panoramic view on a clear day. At the foot of the citadel, an extraordinary labyrinth has been left in the rock by the former quarries. Jean Cocteau used this site as a setting for his film "Orphée", and it has been used for several years now by the "Cathèdrale d'Images" ("Picture Palace") which puts on spectacular son-et-lumière shows.

Lastly, one cannot speak of Les Baux without mentioning L'Oustau de Baumanière, an outstanding gourmet restaurant. ❧

The full spectrum of ochre, the natural wealth of Roussillon.

ROUSSILLON AND THE COLORADO OF PROVENCE

*Stone takes on the shape of a bird,
a spear or a trident.*

What sculptor created this monster of light and darkness?

A part from the Maures and Estérel mountains, Provence is white or grey, carved out of limestone and schist. But in the heart of the Luberon mountains, the landscape is a surprising spectrum of ochre - there are at least seventeen different shades.

A few kilometres from Apt is the hill-top village of Roussillon, whose name reflects the ruddy color of the ochre rock, rich in iron oxides. The town is built with the ochre that makes it powerful mark on the rocks, cliffs, hills, fields and houses. Below the church lie roofs of pink and honey tiles and a maze of winding narrow streets. Local shops make money from ochre. The visitor can buy beautifully presented samples of all the different forms of ochre. Builders exploited the richness of the rock for centuries, probably long before the town was built. Ochre gives the façades their warm tones that glow in all seasons with the slightest ray of sunshine.

The breath-taking red rocks of the Provençal Colorado.

Quarries excavated since the 18th century are now abandoned, leaving a strange landscape of striking beauty. The stone was worked to obtain the precious powder, which was treated in settling ponds. Near the village, we can admire Val des Fées (The Fairies' Valley): it is like a superb setting for a Western, full of caverns, pillars, chasms, needles and ravines shaped out of this dust, to which islands of greenery and pinewoods cling, as if to enhance the dramatic effect. This is a wonderful miniature Colorado on a human scale.

According to a cruel and poetic legend, the land will remain forever soaked in the blood of a woman who did not survive her lover when he was murdered by her jealous husband, Raymond d'Avignon, the local lord. A spring emerges at the place where her body was buried. They say that one of the red cliffs depicts the profile of Raymond

Rolling rows of lavender against a backdrop of snowy crests.

VALENSOLE PLATEAU

The hill-top village of Valensole.

Valensole belongs to the Provence of lavender, that of the more rugged, more austere inland uplands, the birthplace of the stout-hearted characters celebrated by the writer Giono. This large, almost desolate plateau stands to the East of the Durance River near Manosque. One already feels the presence of the Alps. This area is situated on the transhumance routes (used by herds migrating between summer and winter pastures).

For a long time, the almond tree was the area's main source of wealth. In Spring the plain is adorned with a multitude of blossoms. Flat stretches sweep in a slope towards Digne. The cultivation of lavandin and lavender has been developed here since the period between the two World Wars. This floral environment attracts bee-keepers. The market town of Valensole, which is situated in a fold in the plateau, has a population of less than 2,000. The church and the buildings of the former Benedictine priory tower above the steep streets and alleyways furrowed by the flow of water. A strange sort of wild charm emanates from these lonesome heights.

Turned into stone by Fate, the monks of Les Mées continue their motionless procession.

DENTELLES DE MONTMIRAIL AND PENITENTS DES MÉES

Provence is a land of contrasts shaped by the raging Mistral wind and devastating torrential rains. Erosion has sculpted its soft rock and created picturesque beauty spots. Thus, the hamlet of Montmirail between Vacqueyras and Carpentras has a natural curiosity shaped in the rock: its famous "dentelles" (literally "lacework") of finely cut and perforated blades of rock, apparently the handiwork of some giant's wife.

Just a few miles from Digne, on the left bank of the River Durance, is the town of Les Mées, which is famous for its strange rocks composed of a sort of reddish-brown "pudding-stone", some of which reach up to 100 metres high. With their tapered tops and their pyramidal bases, they look like a procession of cloaked monks - hence their name: "The Penitents of Les Mées".

According to a legend dating from the wars with the Saracens, the monks of Saint Donat succumbed to the charms of the beautiful Moorish women who were placed in their care, and they were turned into stone as a punishment. ✎

Stone finery shaped by the hands of fairies: The Dentelles de Montmirail.

THE VERDON GORGES

The picturesque road winds along
the cliffside through the Verdon Gorges.

Opposite:
The river cuts through the awe-inspiring cliffs.

The River Verdon, "the tumultuous fiancé of the Durance", is one of the seven wonders of Provence. This torrential river comes down the Lower Alps and flows into the River Durance 200 kilometres downstream. After Castellane, it enters the famous deep gorges that end at Gréoux-les-Bains, 21 kilometres further downstream. Between these two points, there is a succession of wild beauty spots with breathtaking clefts, overhangs and ledges in the rock, such as the Chasteuil cross valley or the great canyon of Rougon. The Cavaliers Cliff or the famous Balcons de la Mescla, the canyons of Beaudinar and Quinson deserve special mention.

At the bottom of the sheer cliffs flows an emerald stream with sections of rapids. It was this little stream that carved these gigantic natural sculptures. In the Grand Cañon, a site unique in Europe, between Pont Sublime and Le Galetas, it has cut itself a bed one thousand metres deep. Visitors used to shy away from this forbidding landscape. It was the "Devil's Path", with abysses and cliffs cut out of the tormented rocks, where no-one dared to venture. During the Edwardian Era, people began to appreciate this grandiose scenery and to explore it with the aid of an inhabitant of Rougon, Isidor Blanc, and the speleologist Martel (the bottom of the gorges can be explored via a hiking path that bears the latter's name).

These two pioneers were not content to just explore this enormous chasm and to improve its image, firstly in the eyes of the local people; they also turned it into an extraordinary tourist goldmine. Since then, the river has been tamed and the area developed without detriment to its wild beauty. Schemes such as the dams at Salles and Sainte-Croix have added very pleasant lakes and watercourses.

Other attractions include the gorges of the Verdun's tributary, the River Arturby. There is a stunning view from the bridge 180 metres above the river. At the point where the Verdon leaves its gorges for flat fertile land is the thermal spa town of Gréoux-les-Bains, which was already well known in Roman times. ∿

A paradise for water sports enthusiasts.

View of Sainte Baume Mountain.

SAINTE-BAUME
AND SAINT-MAXIMIN

*An oratory beside a forest path reflects
the spirit of the place.*

A sacred mountain and a key place in Provençal mythology, situated on the border between the Bouches-du-Rhone and Var areas, Sainte Baume Mountain owes its name to the cave ("baume" in the Provençal language) excavated at the foot of Saint-Pilon, facing northwards. Mary Magdalene retired to this cave after spreading the Christian Gospel in Provence. It has become a place of pilgrimage and retreat. A footpath lined with oratories leads to the cave.

The Saint Baume mountain range, which reaches a height of more than 1,148 metres

Saint Maximin Basilica:
Fresco detail.

Magdalene - which is justly consider ed the oldest and most remarkable gothic building in Provence - and the adjoining convent. The Dominican philosophy imposed simplicity on the architecture, in keeping with the spirit of the area. The town walls were erected on the orders of King René of Provence to protect the relics of Saint Mary Magdalene that are preserved in the crypt. The Basilica has three naves with chapels, the longest of which measures 72.60 metres.

This is the *"Fenestrado Baselico"* praised by Mistral. There were formerly 66 window openings, but only 44 remain. The apse in seven sections is particularly remarkable. The Basilica is also famous for its organs built on the initiative of the Dominican Isnard and his nephew Joseph. The entire complex has been restored recently and is the venue for many cultural activities, particularly musical, during the summer festivals. ❧

The impressive nave of
Saint-Maximin Basilica.

at Baou Saint Gassien, is a veritable reservoir from which a multitude of streams flow down to irrigate the coastal plains. A wild forest of 140 hectares towers overlooks the cliff. It is a remarkable historical legacy composed of an extraordinary variety of plants, including beech, pine, ash, maple and oak. Holly and yew trees also prosper, as well as ferns. The undergrowth, bathing in an aquarium-like light, is a beautiful sight for walkers. However, Chateaubriand painted a negative picture of the forest: "These trees, which offer their foliage to no breeze, inspire particular horror. Abundant water falls from the black springs and sad, shapeless statues of gods stand artlessly on cut trunks: the mould and pallor on these rotten trees are stunning".

Saint Maximin, built on a former lake at the bottom of the mountain range, is well-known for its Basilica of Saint Mary

Porquerolles, a yachting paradise.

THE LEVANT ISLANDS

The Levant Islands are off the coast from Hyères, the most southerly and one of the oldest seaside resorts on the French Riviera. These "Golden Islands" of Porquerolles, Port Cros, Bagaud and Le Levant are synonymous with sunshine. Three of them are inhabited. There are ferries from Hyères harbour and from the landing stage of Tour-Fondu at the tip of the Giens peninsula. In a beautiful preserved setting, the visitor revels in a paradise of fragrance, colours and tastes.

Port Cros: a rugged beauty preserved.

Azure sky and sea on the island of Port Cros, a model for conservation of the marine environment.

Porquerolles, which was private property until recently, is the closest of the islands. It stretches for eight kilometres from East to West, and is no more than two kilometres wide. Porquerolles got its name from the wild boar that were once abundant on the island. In the area between Cap des Mèdes and the point of Grand Langoustier there are beautiful beaches, the island's only yachting harbor and the village - with its rustic church and its inns - which is the starting point for numerous hiking and cycling paths that pass through lush profuse vegetation. Pine, cypress, mastic-tree, thyme and rosemary are in enchanting harmony with the sky and sea. The south coast is abrupt and jagged.

Play of light and shade: the charm of Porquerolles.

Port Cros is more compact and hilly, resembling a large crab. The sea cliffs on the south side are a haven for sea birds. The island has been a conservation area since 1963 and is the base for the National Park, which also includes the neighbouring island of Bagaud. This nature reserve, where all fishing is prohibited, allows the flora and fauna to renew itself on land and in the sea.

The one kilometre wide Grottes Pass separates Port-Cros from Le Levant Island, whose eight kilometres long rocky crest stands out above the sea. One half of the island is occupied by a French Navy test station. The other is a free area devoted to the Héliopolis naturist centre. The only access to the water's edge is via two calanques (rocky coves). There is a splendid view from Fort Napoléon, which towers above the island. ◠

Tormented landscape of the Maures mountain range.

THE MAURES AND ESTEREL MOUNTAINS

The Maures and Estérel mountain ranges are two of Provence's major tourist attractions. They are the rocky gateways to the French Riviera. The Maures Mountains, composed of granite and schist, are a veritable open-air museum of geology. They got their name from the invasions by the Saracens or Moors. The coast is a succession of picturesque little ports such as Rayol, Cavalaire, Saint-Aygulf and Sainte-Maxime. However, the most famous is Saint-Tropez, which has become legendary.

Situated on the ancient Aurelian Way between the two ranges is Fréjus, which was once a rival of Marseille and now attracts archaeology enthusiasts to its town walls, its citadel, its aqueduct and its Roman amphitheater, which is considered the oldest in Gaul. Fréjus has one of the finest beaches on the coast: no less than five kilometres of fine, golden sand. It holds the keys to the Estérel Mountains. It is the start of what Marcel Brion calls "luxurious Provence", sophisticated and glittering. The vegetation becomes lusher, with a rich mixture of species and a touch of Africa. Here, the coastline truly merits its French name of "Azure Coast". The visitor is dazzled by a profusion of riches.

The Estérel Mountains were named after the good fairy Estello, who is the

The pine tree, the most common tree in the region.

patron saint of the Félibrige (the Provençal literary revival movement). However, the region once had a bad reputation as a hideout of bandits, including Gaspar de Besse and Mandrin, whose stronghold was the Adrets Inn. At the time, people only travelled through the area in organized, escorted convoys. Fortunately, times have changed and tourists can now admire the spectacle of red porphyry and sandstone escarpments that sweep down into the clear blue waters. The dazzling "Corniche d'Or" (Golden Coast Road) starts from Saint-Raphaël and passes through charming holiday resorts such as Boulouris, Agay, Anthéor, Théoule and La Napoule, before reaching Cannes, famous for its palatial hotels and its festivals. ❧

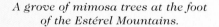

A grove of mimosa trees at the foot of the Estérel Mountains.

Les Maures and Estérel mountain ranges: General view.

A "great Greco-Latin garden" overlooked by Sainte Victoire Mountain.

THE AIX COUNTRYSIDE

by Jacqueline de Romilly.

The little church....

Jacqueline de Romilly, who was born in Chartres, is our most famous Greek scholar. A professor of College de France, elected to the French Academy, she has written many important books.
My husband has a house in the Aix countryside. I go there for all my holidays.
The Aix countryside is my real homeland.

... and Le Tholonet's only café.

*In the footsteps
of the great artist.*

"**I** mention this house and local walks in my book about the footpaths of Mount Sainte Victoire. I love its grandeur. We enjoy the same light and the same sun as the Riviera, but with more great open spaces, in a vast landscape where nature flourishes freely. The scenery does not change greatly from one season to the next because the pines and many other trees do not lose their leaves.

This creates an impression of greenery and life. There are wild flowers that are unique to the area, and I know all their secrets. I especially love the southern slope of Sainte Victoire and the reflected light

Just off the path: Cezanne's windmill.

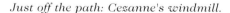

on the bright limestone. Sainte Victoire is the focal point of all landscape in the area. It offers countless pleasant walks, which are unfortunately forbidden in summer due to the risk of fire. I have travelled a lot. I know Greece well, with its great olive-trees that make those of Provence seem so small.

But when I return to the Aix country side, I always have the same impression of grandeur and peace. I also love the villages of Provence, the country houses, the clock towers and the markets where the light plays on the colourful fruit and vegetables. At Le Tholonet, where I live, there is a moment of exquisite splendor when the Judas trees are in bloom. It has all the atmosphere of the villages of the South, with its little church and its one shaded café."

(From an interview)

HERITAGE, TOWNS AND
VILLAGES OF PROVENCE

Aix-en-Provence: The Provençal market in front of the belfry.

AIX-EN-PROVENCE

*Atlante at
Hôtel de Maurel de Pontevès.*

*Previous pages:
Le Tholonnet in
its green setting has
inspired many painters.*

Strolling around Aix, the visitor is charmed by its wonderful mellow gracefulness. The former Roman town of Aquae Sextae was first famous for the quality of its spas. When Aix was King René's capital and seat of the parliament of Provence, water remained an important feature of the town. Its many beautiful fountains have never ceased to sing in the numerous squares all around the town centre. The large bowl of the Rotonde fountain greets

An example of Aix's refinement: the aristocratic Vendôme Pavilion.

the arriving visitor and opens the perspective onto Cours Mirabeau, the town's finest avenue, 440 metres long, which runs along one side of the old town, with fountains at regular intervals and four rows of planes trees. Always busy, it is lined with elegant mansions such as the Hôtel de Maurel de Pontèves and cafés such as the world-famous "Les Deux Garçons".

The most remarkable square is without doubt Place d'Albertas, but the squares at the Town Hall and the Clock Tower are also marvellous. The finest buildings include the Vendôme Pavilion (built by Louis de Mercoeur, Duke of Vendôme, for the "beauty from Le Canet"), Hôtel du Poët, Hôtel de Caumont (which houses the Music Conservatory), Hôtel Boyer d'Eguilles (which houses the Natural History Museum), and Hôtel de Chateaurenard and its remarkable stairway decorated with a baroque "trompe-l'oeil". Saint Sauveur Cathedral (where one can admire Nicolas Froment's triptych of "The Burning Bush") and its cloister are symbols of the Aix people's religious architecture and their faith. Nearby is the Palais de l'Archevêché (Archbishop's Palace), a focal point of the Aix Music Festival, which is dedicated to Mozart. After being considered a sleeping beauty withdrawn behind its fine mansions and its elegant facades, Aix has evolved without losing its soul. Its youth, spirit and taste are sustained by the many students that attend the University, by tourists from all over the world, and by music lovers and artists. All of which makes Aix-en-Provence an immensely appealing town of incomparable charm. ∾

View of Saint Sauveur Cathedral from the cloister.

Ruins of Glanum: The ancient columns now bear only the sky and the weight of history.

SAINT-RÉMY-DE-PROVENCE

by
Françoise Bon

*The smiling faces of the Alpilles:
Françoise Bon and her girls.*

*A village
where life is good.*

*F*rançoise Bon has been living in Saint Rémy de Provence for twenty years. She chairs the local Tourist Office and owns the hotel "Le Château des Alpilles", an early 19th century country house that was a meeting-place for politicians and writers of the time, such as Chateaubriand, Lamartine and Thiers. Her select hotel welcomes patrons like special guests.

Market day on the town hall square.

Saint Remy de Provence is one of Provence's greatest tourist attractions.the village is not just a single street: it is built on a round plan. One just has to stop and visit it. There is a really harmonious atmosphere, with a high quality of life and a special kind of light. Saint Remy is a well-situated crossroads in a region of festivals, near the sea and the mountains.

Many artists have come here to live. Those who developed the town have managed to make it into a major tourist attraction. There are two parts to the town: a dry area - La Galine - and another area, which is greener and more lush. I particularly love the parks and gardens, with their countless shades of green. Saint Remy is an ideal base for discovering the Alpilles Hills on foot or on bicycle. And one must not forget the ancient remains of the Glanum site, the Roman Mausoleum and Commemorative Arch, which are a "must" for tourists or lovers of archaeology. The Tourist Office is trying to extend the season while keeping a fine balance between local life and tourism. Saint Remy is rather like the Saint-Tropez of thirty years ago. ∿

Ruins of Glanum: The mausoleum and the triumphal arch, images of Roman grandeur.

The village of Gordes stands around the castle on its promontory.

GORDES

by Elisabeth Bourgeois

The famous village of Les Bories preserves the dry stone dwellings of our distant ancestors.

Paris-born Elisabeth Bourgeois arrived in Provence at the age of fourteen. In her heart, in her way of living and working, in putting across her culinary message, she feels that she is a Provencal woman. For eleven years, in the Gordes countryside, she has been running "Le Mas Tourteron", which Peter Mayle lists as one of his favourite eating-places.

Gordes is listed as one of "the most beautiful villages in France". It was built with the stone of the rock on which it perches, from where there is a wonderful view. I love Senanque Abbey, where I never miss Midnight Mass; the village of "bories" (stone shepherds' huts), an historic monument dating from the Bronze Age; and the chateau that is now used as the town hall - it no longer houses the Vasarely Museum.

Gordes has a museum of stained glass and the history of glass, a lavender museum, and Moulin des Bouillons, the oldest intact oil press in existence. In the summer a festival of theatre, classical music and jazz is held on the "terraces" above the rocks, with a view of the Luberon Mountains. Unfortunately, my husband and I cannot attend because of our work in the restaurant. "Le Mas Tourteron" is typically Provencal. Food is cooked mainly by women, using local produce. ⌁

Roussillon village stands like an extension of the land that bears it.

THE MOST BEAUTIFUL VILLAGES OF THE LUBERON

by The Duc d'Orléans

The Duke of Orléans, a descendant of France's royal family, has travelled around the Luberon Mountains for thirty years. He has explored most of the paths in the area on horseback, on a donkey and on foot to pursue his keen interest in photography. Here he talks of the villages that he considers the most beautiful.

A Looking for unusual subjects for my photographs, I discovered the real Luberon, with its little villages where people still speak in the Provençal language. When you go to these villages by foot along country roads and lanes, you see them from a different point of view and discover hidden treasures. During one of my rambles, I came across a pretty little church called Notre Dame des Anges near Cadenet. It was rebuilt with stones from demolished convents, which had been built previously in this place that lends itself to meditation. An inscription above the door says: "*Si dans ton coeur le nom de Marie est gravé, souviens-toi en passant de lui dire un Ave*" ("If the name of Mary is engraved in your heart, remember to say an Ave Maria in passing").

The church of Oppède-le-Vieux towers above the wild vales.

The houses of Saignon around the natural fortress dismantled by the centuries.

Like Ansouis, the fort of Buoux was a Roman oppidum. It is a magical place. People lived in the rocks in the 17th century. There are still traces of habitation.

Cucuron is a fortified village whose town walls still exist. At each end of the town there are two gates on which the portcullises left indelible marks. History is everywhere in this village. One can very easily imagine how it was hundreds of years ago. The three public wash-houses are still intact, as is the large pond surrounded by enormous plane trees which collected the rainwater of the southern Luberon for the oil presses. It is an enclosed village that managed to keep out the plague. In thanksgiving, the people built a little chapel called the Hermitage on top of the mountain. Every year, the "May Tree procession" is held on the first Sunday of May: the men of the village go and look for a poplar tree that is tall enough to reach the church bell-tower. The film *"Le Hussard sur le toit"* was filmed on location in Cucuron.

Cucuron, a village steeped in history.

*Above: Beaumont de Pertuis,
wrapped around its hill like a stone snail.*

*Top right:
Bonnieux, one of the key places
in the Luberon area.*

*Above: All the charm of Lourmarin
bathed in glowing sunlight.*

Vaugines, Saignon and Grambois are lovely villages of unique charm. I had trouble reaching Sivergues on foot, but it was well worth it: this typically Provençal village, with only five houses and a little town hall, is breathtakingly beautiful. On the historic road of Claparèdes Plateau, the houses and churches of the Vaudois Christian dissenters were all fortified because of religious persecution, and are steeped in their turbulent past.

Going along the road from La Combe de Lourmarin to Apt, the vegetation changes. There are the pretty villages of Le Castellet, Auribeau, Saint-Martin de la Brasque and Murs. The local farmers tell a legend about Murs: Three hundred years ago, the lord of the castle fell in love with a young girl from a nearby village. He had a splendid avenue of oak trees planted between the two villages so that he would have shade on his way to meet his true love. It is thus that I have felt a real local identity on my travels in the area. I know the local people well - they often see me scouring the countryside with my camera. They are the soul and memory of the villages of Provence. ∽

Fontaine de Vaucluse:
Laure and Petrarch gazed at their
reflections in these crystal-clear waters.

Fontaine de Vaucluse:
The mystery of the springing stream.

FONTAINE-DE-VAUCLUSE AND L'ISLE-SUR LA-SORGUE

by Michel Mélanie

Born in L'Isle-sur-la-Sorgue, where his family has been living since 1800, Mr Mélamie chairs the Kayak-Vert Society. For more than ten years, he has helped others to share his love of nature by organising canoe and kayak expeditions and trout fishing on the River Sorgue.

For years, divers have tried to unfold the mystery of the "Fontaine de Vaucluse", the resurgent spring that is the source of the River Sorgue. Apparently, it results from the confluence of a series of potholes that form an underground lake, which explains the area's abundant supply of water. Tourism has now replaced paper milling as the main economic activity in the valley. Walkers can follow special trails to discover the surrounding villages and the hills of the Vaucluse area.

The Sorgue is a first class river: there is no artificial introduction of farmed fish, since fish breed naturally in the river. By agreement with the fishing authorities, there is no canoeing or kayaking until the third weekend in April. The village is marvellous, with its church and castle. Its pleasant shade provides a welcome haven from the summer heat. There are several museums on themes such as the French Resistance, the Paper industry, Petrarch, or the "Subterranean World" visitor centre devoted to speleology, which is run by Norbert Casteret in the Campredon Mansion House. With its many little canals and wharves, L'Isle-sur-la-Sorgue truly deserves its name of "Venise comtadine" (Venice of the Comtat area)...~

The Lord of the Luberon: Lourmarin Castle, a major arts centre, where Henri Bosco reigned.

THE CASTLES OF THE LUBERON MOUNTAINS

Lourmarin Castle:
Detail. Mellow, harmonious balance.

The Luberon Mountains extend for 65 km from around Manosque to Cavaillon. Two very different valleys pass through them: the Coulon (or Calavon) Valley in the North, an austere area of ravines and copses; and the Durance Valley in the South, with its rich and fertile land used for market gardening. There are castles everywhere in this region - indeed, they make up a veritable tourist trail - but they are more numerous and more interesting in the southern part. In some cases, only ruins remain, while others are open to the public or are even still inhabited. I will

The impressive skyline of La Tour d'Aigues Castle stands out above the vineyards.

deliberately mention only those that are located within the boundaries of the present Luberon Regional Park. They mark and divide up the historic trail of the "Vaudois" (or "Waldenses", a movement of Christian dissenters dating from the 12th century) whose memory still remains in many places.

The square keep of Ansouis Castle towers above the village. There are still some remains of the original feudal fortress. However, there is a very classical air about the terraces planted with trees and bushes that lead to the elegant aristocratic 17th century buildings. The well-restored complex still belongs to the Sabran-Pontèves family. The castle of Tour d'Aigues is like an extraordinary unfinished stage set. It seems like it was created for a play or an historic film that was never completed. It occupies a large four-sided area on the village square. The Roman keep rises in the centre and two corner wings frame a monu-

La Tour d'Aigues Castle:
A neoclassical gateway opens
on to peaceful solitude.

mental entrance gate that is surmounted by a triangular pediment. This astonishing mixture of ancient and Renaissance styles is well worth a detour.

The shadow of the Marquis de Sade still hangs over the ruins of Lacoste Castle, which is perched at the top of the village of the same name. Sade lived in the castle before being imprisoned in the Bastille. After being sacked during the wars of religion and during the French Revolution, it has been

Above:
The memory of the heretical Marquis de Sade
haunts the ruins of Lacoste Castle.

Opposite:
Lauris Castle overlooks
the Alpilles Hills from the top of its promontory.

restored for the last forty years by an amateur connoisseur.

The fort of Oppède-le-Vieux dates from the 12th century. Its ruins are listed as a historic monument. Like many similar buildings, it was rebuilt during the Renaissance, when Humanism appreciated the true value of cultural heritage. After being abandoned during the French Revolution, its stones were taken for building elsewhere. Its gaunt, ghostly form dominates the site like a tormented witness to the horrors of the past.

Buoux Castle, with its tall Renaissance buildings, stands in splendid isolation in a wooded vale. It has a melancholic air that invites one to look more closely. It is well worth making the effort to explore such a fine old building.

Local scholars and men of knowledge used to meet in Lourmarin Castle. This is the Provence of Bosco, and also the Provence of Camus, who lived in the village and is buried in the local cemetery. The castle is now managed by an association that continues the old tradition by hosting writers and artists-in-residence.

THE ABBEYS
OF PROVENCE

There are many abbeys in Provence, characterized by their austere, serene beauty. Four kilometres from Arles is Montmajour Abbey. After being burned in 1726, then handed over to the State during the French Revolution, it has been partly restored. In a hollow of the Montagnette Hills nestles Saint-Michel-de-Frigolet, which Daudet made famous in his "Letters from My Mill". Its name comes from *"ferigoulo"*, the Provençal word for thyme. The folklorist Marie Mauron sings of the *"fragrant path that rises through its peaceful foliage"*.

Aiguebelle Trappist monastery, in a cheerful vale of the Drôme region, fully deserves its name, which means "beautiful water". Above Collobrières, the Charterhouse of La Verne is a haven of peace surrounded by chestnut trees. However, it is the "three Cistercian sisters" that attract the most attention: the abbeys of Sénanque, Silvacane and Le Thoronet. They are built in accordance with principles dictated by their Order. The cloister is central, serving the church and all the buildings. The beauty of these abbeys is derived from their compliance with the Order's Rule. Built in the middle of the 12th century, they retain the strict Romanesque style combined with the beginnings of the Gothic style.

Near Gorde, the clear, bare outline of Sénanque Abbey (founded 1148) stands out against a backdrop of lavender. It is the

Le Thoronet Abbey:
One of the "Three Cistercian Sisters"
of Provence.

most cheerful of the "three sisters" because of its setting and the fine arrangement of its white stone cloister. Monks have been living in the abbey again in recent years. In the woodland beside the abbey, the visitor can admire a six hundred year old oak tree.

Silvacane Abbey (founded 1147) got its name from the cane that grows nearby. This masterpiece of religious architecture in a very pure, well-proportioned Cistercian style was restored after a tumultuous history. The architects gave priority to austerity and a solemn appearance that were conducive to meditation. Concerts are held in the Abbey as part of the Roque d'Anthéron Festival.

Le Thoronet (founded 1146) lies on a forest road between Brignoles and Vidauban. This abbey built by the monks and lay brothers is considered the finest and the most austere. Made of pink and red stone, it is in the pure Romanesque style, except for the Gothic chapter house. It is a model of the Order's esoteric architecture - as François Galli says: *"an immense sundial where the concrete observation of the Hours found its liturgical legend and its mystical significance in each part of the Divine Office"*. ∽

Montmajour.Abbey:
view of the Abbey Tower
from the cloister.

Opposite:
The cloister of
Senanque Abbey.

Insert:
Like a floral procession, the
rows of lavender converge
on Sénanque Abbey.

Vaison-la-Romaine and the ancient bridge over the Ouvèze .

VAISON-LA-ROMAINE
by Daniel Ceccaldi

Daniel Ceccaldi, a well-known French actor, has family roots half in Corsica and half in the Paris region but, above all, he feels Mediterranean. He fell in love with the Drome region during the shooting of the film "Le Chaud Lapin". It was at that time also that he first discovered Seguret, near

A man in love with Vaison-la-Romaine: Daniel Ceccaldi.

Vaison-la-Romaine, where he had a house built in 1980. Since then he divides his time between Paris and his Drome country house.

Vaison-la-Romaine: Puymin ruins & statue of Sabine.

A fountain makes time stand still on a square.

I knew the Luberon region long before settling near Vaison. Forty years ago its villages were deserted, but at the time I did not have enough money to settle there. Later on, a friend invited me to join him in the Luberon, but in between times I had discovered Vaison, where I find the countryside more graceful. It reminds me of Tuscany, with its cypress trees, which are typical of the region around Florence. The two regions have exactly the same climate.

The colours here are different from those of the Riviera and the Luberon region. The countryside is both very rugged and very mellow. The real Provençal people are not as easygoing as one is led to believe - in fact, they can be quite hot-tempered. While outwardly they may appear welcoming and friendly, they are actually distrustful and jealously possessive of their region. If you live here long enough, they accept you, but it takes a long time. The town of Vaison is sublime. It is made up of a lower town, which was built by the Romans, and the upper town dating from Medieval times. There is a Roman bridge that spans the River Ouveze and links the upper and lower parts.

Anywhere you dig a hole here, you come across Roman remains. It is the most important archaeological site in France, with an extremely rich store of treasures. It is the mixture of styles and ruins that gives Vaison its charm. I am particularly fond of Place Monfort and its *café* fronts, especially in spring and autumn. I live nearby in Seguret. From my house, I have an absolutely magnificent view of Sablet, Rasteau and the church at Cairanne and, on a clear night, the lights of Avignon and Nimes. Spread all around is a countryside filled with vineyards whose colors vary from season to season. I dearly love Paris but I spend several days in Vaison every month. I always tell the locals how lucky they are to live in such a beautiful place. ✍

Vaison's houses are stacked up on the hillside in an atmosphere reminiscent of Tuscany.

SISTERON AND GANAGOBIE

by Louis Heyries

Sisteron, the gateway to the Dauphiné region, marks the boundary of the olive-growing area at the northern edge of Provence. The once turbulent River Durance, now tamed by a hydroelectric dam, flows past the town. Sisteron is a stopping-place on the way to the south coast and the ski resorts. It has many interesting historic monuments and buildings: the Citadel, the cathedral of Notre Dame des Pommiers ("Our Lady of the Apple-Trees"), the monasteries and the town walls. From the top of the Citadel, which was built in the 12th, 16th and 19th centuries, there is a striking view covering 100 kilometres, including the Durance Valley and La Baume Rock. After being damaged in the bombardment of 1944, it has been restored since 1956 by the ATM association under the aegis of the town council and the Historic Monuments Authority, and is a major tourist attraction. The 10th century Priory of Ganagobie is a few kilometres from Sisteron on the plateau of the same name that overlooks the Durance. Listed as a Historic Building in 1946, it is now occupied by twenty monks who grow lavender, olives and almonds and organize religious retreats. ✍

On the doorstep of Provence: the impressive citadel of Sisteron.

La Baume Rock, from the opposite side of the Durance.

Bendor Island combines tourism and the arts.

Bandol harbor has preserved its charm despite the development of the marina.

BANDOL

by Alain Bombard

Alain Bombard is a doctor and biologist, a yachtsman famous for his voluntary castaway experiment, an honorary Member of the European Parliament, founder of the Iles des Embiez scientific complex, and author of several books. Although born in Paris, he has become one of Provence's leading personalities. He has chosen to live in Bandol.

I was fourteen years old when I discovered Provence. I travelled from Marseille to Menton with my father. I have been coming to Provence for thirty years and I having been living here for fourteen years. I have decided to live the rest of my days here. I have become more Provencal than Parisian. You cannot live in Provence if you do not love it.

From Marseille to Toulon, the Mediterranean coats full of splendid bays and hills, in contrast with the flat monotony of Languedoc. It is dotted with ports such as Saint-Cyr, Bandol and Sanary, as far as Cap Sicie. The ever-busy sailing resort of Bandol attracts all lovers of the sea: painters, writers, yachtsmen and travellers in search of beauty. The sea is the backdrop for all the hills: it is very alive, changing all the time. There is a wonderful view of the town from off the coast. The houses blend perfectly with the landscape. Welcome to Bandol! Taste the pleasure of living and admire the beauty of nature! ∼

A "cruise" from the Town Hall to Place aux Huiles.

MARSEILLE : THE "FERRY-BOAT"

On June 3rd 1880, a curious boat service was started in Marseille. Strangely enough, it had an English name: the "ferry-boat". Being not very familiar with the English language, the people of Marseille distorted the name with their strong local accent, and it soon became known as the "fériboîte". No-one could have imagined how this modest vessel was to become part of the city's heritage as much as the Basilica of Notre-Dame (otherwise known as "la Bonne Mère") and the Château d'If. The ferry took passengers for the short 206 metres trip from one side of Marseille's Old

Harbour to the other. There were once two services. Now there is only one boat that shuttles back and forth every day between the Town Hall and Place aux Huiles for the sake of tradition. The only current it has ever had to face is the local people's relentless flow of chatter.

However, on August 23rd 1984, it actually sank... filled with rain! It almost disappeared for ever in 1983, when the owners nailed a sign to the landing stage, saying "Closed for good". The people of Marseille were so upset that the "fériboîte" service was resumed in 1985 under the colours of the city with the help of public subsidy. This little boat, which is now over 100 years old, has been immortalised in a trilogy of films by Marcel

Balcony looking onto the "Vieux Port".

Pagnol. It has inspired painters, photographers, writers and also cartoonists such as the inimitable Dubout. No tour of Marseille would be complete without a trip on the ferry. Happy couples board at Place aux Huiles to get married at the Town Hall on the other side. Even the eminent members of the Goncourt Academy once went on a memorable crossing. So it is not surprising that the "fériboîte" is as much part of our popular mythology as the ships of Ulysses and Columbus or great ocean liners such as the "Normandie" and the "Titanic". It has a special place in the hearts of the local people, who are well known for revelling in fantastic exaggeration. ⤳

The "ferry-boat" crosses the Lacydon "ocean".

TRADITIONAL FARE AND
PRODUCTS OF PROVENCE

The fish market: a celebration of the Mediterranean.

A TASTE
OF MARSEILLE

Previous pages:
Emblems of the high plateaux of Provence:
the sickle and the bag of lavender.

The fishwife, a typical Marseille character.

Marseille is known for its famous sights: the Basilica of Notre Dame de la Garde, the Old Harbour, the Chateau d'If and the Canebiere. Everyone knows its historic buildings and monuments: the Garden of Ruins, the Abbey of St Victor, the forts of St Jean and St Nicolas, and Vieille Charite. It is famous for its eminent figures: the architect Pierre Puget, Monsignor Belsunce, Chevalier Roze, the French Revolutionary battalion of Marseille volunteers, the writer and film-maker Pagnol and the characters of his famous trilogy. But a town like this, founded 2,600 years ago, is also known for its culinary delicacies. Naturally, Marseille has much in common with the cuisine of Provence, based on vegetables, fish, olive oil and aromatic herbs. However, it also has its own local specialities that are a delight to discover: pastis, bouillabaisse, pieds et paquets, navettes, panisses and chichi fregi.

Ever since Paul Ricard perfected his magic formula, pastis has become the established drink of Marseille people. This anise aperitif becomes cloudy when cold water is added. It is synonymous with the South of France, summer and sweet idleness. Its connoisseurs take it barely diluted in small glasses, nicknamed "mummies". They are very fussy about their choice of brand. God help anyone who serves a Casanis instead of a Ricard, or a Pernod instead of a Jeannot, or vice versa. Pastis lends itself to different flavourings: with a little mint cordial it becomes a "perroquet" ("*parrot*"), just a touch of grenadine turns it into a "tomate", or a drop of orgeat changes it into a "mauresque".

The "Good Mother" keeps a watchful eye on the city's gastronomic reputation.

Bouillabaisse (from the Provencal "*boui-abaisso*") was originally a poor person's dish cooked by fishermen to use up unsold fish. It has now becomea luxury because the recipe requires a lot of different rockfish, each with its own particular taste: rascasse (*hog-fish*), galinette, vive (*stingfish*), roucaou, saint-pierre (*John Dory*) and conger eel. The main difficulty is in varying the cooking times of all the types of fish so that they are all presentable. The name comes from the cooking technique: "when it boils (*bouille*), turn down the heat (*abaisse*)". Bouillabaisse is served with rouille (paste of pimento, saffron and garlic) and garlic croutons onto which the thin soup is poured. Restaurant owners of Marseille have signed a "Bouillabaisse Charter" to ensure the authentic quality of this dish. Pieds et paquets marseillais are made with stewed mutton tripe (stuffed with mince and rolled into paupiettes) and mutton trotters, according to a local recipe that is detailed in the region's cookbooks. This dish is greatly prized by connois-

The great spans of the Rove Aqueduct just beside l'Estaque, the birthplace of "panisses" and "chichis-fregis".

The "Four des Navettes" bakery, guardian of a centuries-old tradition.

seurs. Panisses ("*panisso*") are made from a paste of chickpea flour that is shaped into a roll, then cut into round slices and fried. They are best when golden brown and crisp-fried. Navettes ("*noveto de Sant-Vitou*") are dry biscuits made according to a secret formula in the shape of a boat, symbolizing the boat in which the two Saint Marys are said to have landed in Provence. They are made in Marseille's oldest bakery. Lastly, the chichi fregi, a delicious long thin twisted fritter rolled in sugar, has now become a rarity. ∾

The glorious colors and smells of fruit and vegetables in the markets of Provence.

THE MARKETS OF PROVENCE:
AT THE GATEWAY TO THE ORIENT

by Odile Godard

A trickle of olive oil on some bread:
the taste of Provence.

In the morning, the town centre comes to life early. There is a feverish atmosphere in the square and in the neighbouring streets; it is market day. The stallholders unpack trestles, tabletops and canopies, and set up the scenery of the theatre where the same drama is enacted one morning every week, with the traders, their goods and the customers as the leading actors. And what actors! Everyone has their own speciality and applies the same artful skill in staging this gourmet festival with the assistance of the shoppers.

There is the greengrocer whose colourful assortment of freshly-picked fruit and vegetables is a splendid painter's palette. There are rows of dishes full of all sorts of olives, anchovies and dried fruit, against a backdrop of salted cod and strings of garlic. At the next stall, a young farmer's wife presents a large basket of eggs laid by her hens, some goat cheese and the season's fresh fruit from her orchards: walnuts, strawberries, cherries or peaches.

"Chez Gracieuse" in the heart of Marseille.

Further on is the poultry seller, who is busy cleaning and trussing cocks, chickens, guinea-fowl, rabbits or perhaps the Easter kid goat, under the watchful eyes of skilled cooks who know exactly what they are looking for. And there is the friendly gardener who has set up her wares on the pavement: trays of flowering plants or *fines herbes* ready for replanting in one's garden. People stop to admire them and dream, even if they have only a small balcony on the third floor of an apartment block. Then there is the fish merchant's corner: people flock to it and wait while the merchant entertains the crowd, usually at the expense of those who pass by his stall. An old lady makes the mistake of grumbling as she walks past a bucket full of waste fish:

The authenticity of Aubagne's market.

"The cats are going to have a treat!", to which the fish merchant instantly retorts: "I've fed a helluva lot of cats in my time! Anyway, I'd rather feed a cat than a woman: it costs a lot less!". The customers burst out laughing, while the old lady pretends not to hear and moves on.

The stimulating smells excite the taste buds, particularly as lunch-time draws near. A chef sets up his street stall and cooks *paella*, frittered shrimps, spring rolls or lamb *tajine* as passing shoppers watch, their mouths watering. You could almost be in a souk or an oriental bazaar.

Colours, aromas, fresh produce, everything to delight the gourmet, pleasant chat and *joie de vivre* - these are the things that attract people to the markets of Provence. In the good weather, people stroll around in the shade, taking their time, chatting, swapping recipes and joking, and then they return home feeling light-hearted, their baskets full of wonderful treasures.

The truffle, the black diamond of gastronomy.

THE TRUFFLE

by Guy Monnier

Chair of the "Maison de la Truffe" in Paris, Guy Monnier has worked tirelessly to introduce the uninitiated public to the taste of the truffle, sharing the secrets of its storage and cooking in his book "Les bonnes recettes de la truffe".

When the Popes moved to Provence, John XXII, bishop of Cahors, planted the first truffle-producing oaks from the Périgord. Since then, the Tuber melanosporum has become the black diamond of the Haut Vaucluse area, rare and highly appreciated for its outstanding sweet flavour.

Truffle growing depends on the climate and requires a lot of patience and know-how. Truffle oaks produce the first crops about twenty years after being planted. Gathered with the help of dogs or pigs, Tricastin truffles are sold at the markets in Carpentras, Valréas and Richerenches (which is listed as a "site du goût" - a place of outstanding gastronomy). There are a lot of traditions, customs and mysticism related to the growing and trading of truffles. In January the members of the "Brotherhood of the Black Diamond" gather in their black capes and hats, with a black-striped yellow ribbon round their necks, at a special mass in Richerenches. The local people give truffles as offerings to gain the protection of Saint Anthony. Their truffles are then sold by auction on the village square after a long procession. ⌇

Olive-grove in the Alpilles Hills.

OLIVE OIL
by Christian Rossi

*Christian Rossi, a miller in
Mouries, chairs the association of olive-
press operators of Les Baux Valley.*

Picking olives.

*Basket of
freshly-picked olives.*

The olive-tree is a very generous tree, a tree of peace and eternity, because it never dies. It symbolizes Provence and the countries of the Mediterranean. There are two main categories of olive oil. Virgin olive oils have undergone no chemical processing, and are obtained only by mechanical processes. This category includes "*vierge extra*" ("extra virgin" olive oil) - which has very low acidity - and normal "*huile vierge*" ("virgin" olive oil). Ordinary olive oil is produced by blending virgin oil and refined oil. Oil has to be imported into France because it produces only 2% of its olive oil consumption. There is a growing fashion for olive oil because of its fine taste and its beneficial properties for health and beauty care.

In the Alpilles Hills, traditional techniques are still used to make olive oil of a

high quality that cannot be obtained by the large-scale production of other countries. Production is mainly on a small scale. People like Jean Reno who have two or three olive-trees in their gardens bring me their crop. My olive-press is in Mouries, France's leading producer of olive oil. It would kill me if I had to leave Les Baux Valley. ⌒

A simple treat: "suc de Minerve"
with slices of fresh bread.

Above:
Banon goat cheese ready for tasting.

Left:
Banon: Making goat cheese.

BANON GOAT CHEESE

by Georges Dessaud

Georges Dessaud, a native of Banon, former deputy Mayor, was originally a farmer. He knows everything about goat cheese because his mother used to make it.

The village of Banon, which got its name from the hill that towers above it, was built after invasions by the Moors and Saracens. Cheese has been made in the area ever since it has been inhabited. Situated in a hollow of the "Alpes de Lumiere" with a micro-climate, Banon has a high level of sunshine. The mid-mountain landscape is dotted with fields of lavender. The soil is quite dry with a high limestone content. An infinite variety of herbs and plants give the local milk and cheese their unique taste. The milk is soured and refined, then the cheese is wrapped in chestnut leaves (collected in the autumn) and stored in earthenware jars or, for small quantities, between two plates.

Banon cheese has no need of additives: it is complete in itself. It is sold in three forms: the "fresh *tomme*", the "*moelleuse*" (soft cheese) and the "*pliée*" (wrapped in a leaf). Banon cheese has been made with the same technique for 2,000 years. However, with the introduction of European standards, the cheese is now practically never made in the farms themselves, but in a cheese dairy that collects the milk. Our region has thus lost a part of its identity. ✍

Lavender Festival in Sault.

LAVENDER
by José-Luis Adrian

Jose-Luis Adrian was born in Marseille. He became interested in lavender at an early age as he followed his father around the plantations of Provence. With twenty-five years experience in the lavender trade, he is managing director of the Adrian company, one of the leading firms in the essential oils market.

Countryside around Aurel, under the watchful eye of Mount Ventoux.

One must make a distinction between lavender and lavandin. Lavender represents an annual sales figure of 20 million francs and 25 tonnes of output from an area of 2,000 hectares; lavandin has a sales figure of 150 million francs and 1,200 tonnes of output from an area of 6,000 hectares. Lavender, a wild plant cultivated by man, grows on poor land at altitudes of 800 metres or more. It grows best on the Albion Plateau, which produces 60% of French output. It is associated with the writer Giono and with Lure Mountain, where there are fine stone shepherds' huts similar to the famous bories. The farmers in this region face strong competition from Eastern Europe. I work in close cooperation with these farmers in a spirit of partnership. Lavender growing is now a real industrial trade that requires modernized distilling processes.

Lavandin grows on Valensole Plateau at lower altitudes. It is a hybrid produced by cross-fertilization of lavender and aspic (spike lavender). Lavender is mainly used for perfume, whereas lavandin is used for large-scale industrial purposes, e.g. for

The village of Auribeau under an azure sky.

washing powders, detergents and fabric softeners. Therefore it requires considerable modernization of installations. In the 1950's, crops were collected by hand for a period of two months. Nowadays harvesting is mechanized and takes only two or three weeks. In July, before harvesting begins, the countryside is superb with the alternating colours of vibrant blue lavender, yellow corn and the azure sky. The future of lavender is in our hands. We have to rediscover it and develop its use. Efforts have been made, such as the creation of the "Lavender Route" theme trail. Personally, I try to bring the perfume makers to see the plantations as often as possible, because lavender has an unforgettable smell that marks you deeply.

In the Châteauneuf vineyards.

The château built by the Popes.

THE WINES OF CHATEAUNEUF-DU-PAPE

by Jean Abeille

Château Mont-Redon has been a family business for three generations. It was bought in 1923 by the grandfather of Jean Abeille, who now manages it with his brother and his cousin. The property covers 163 hectares, including 100 hectares of vineyards, making it one of the largest estates producing Châteauneuf-du-Pape wine.

A very specific soil.

Châteauneuf wine cellar: An oak cask in which the famous wine of the Popes is matured.

The Popes set up residence in Avignon in the 13th century, and Pope John XXII had his summer residence built in Châteauneuf in the 15th century. This boosted the development of wine-growing, and the Church benefited greatly from it. Our wine is grown in a very specific *"terroir"*, composed of large rounded pebbles of glacial origin. The higher ground, composed of stone terraces two metres high, was the former bed of the River Rhône.

The pebbles store the heat during the day and release it at night, thus ensuring continuous maturing of the grapes. The rolling, wooded Châteauneuf landscape is mainly composed of vineyards separated by high ground, woodland and scrubland. Only 6% of the wine is white - called "Mass wine" - and 94% is red. We use thirteen grape varieties (eight for red, five for white), creating a rich aromatic complexity.

Châteauneuf-du-Pape wine is one of the top five wines under the certified Côtes du Rhône *"appellation"*, and ranks second in terms of surface area. Certain châteaux such as La Nerthe, Fines Roches, Fortia and Vaudieu stand out in the landscape. Châteauneuf-du-Pape is a part of Provence's way of life. ∽

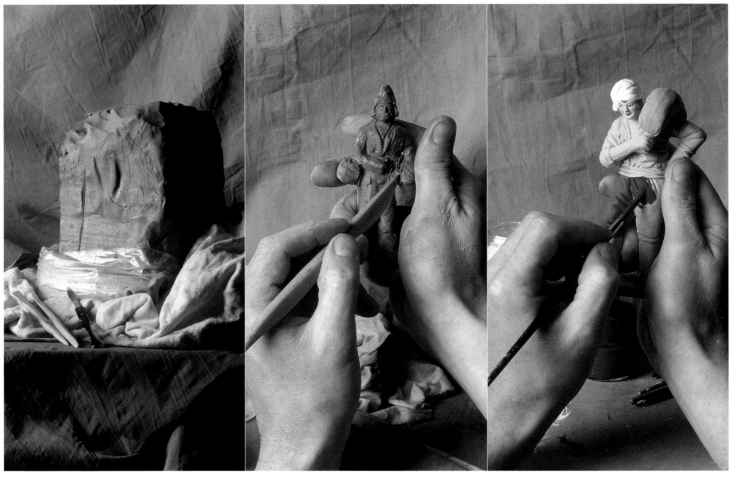

"The santon makers play God the Father".

THE SANTONS

by Philippe Renoux

The tabor drum player.

The hunter.

Santons *symbolize Provence. They reflect the soul of its people. These traditional Christmas crib figurines were first created by Jean-Louis Lagnel from Marseille (1764-1822). They spread throughout Provence during the 20th century. One of the most famous makers is the Carbonel firm.*

Contrary to popular belief, the capital of the *santon* is not Aubagne, but Marseille. Santons appeared after 1789, when people were forbidden to celebrate the Roman Catholic Mass. Marseille families used them to celebrate Christmas Midnight Mass in their homes. The tradition then spread throughout Provence. The Carbonel firm started business in Marseille in 1935. The grandfather, from Marseille, handed over the firm to his daughter, Mme Renoux, in 1977. It was taken over in 1989 by the grandson, who had worked in the firm since the age of fifteen. In the workshops, he supervised the complete traditional product-

The crib with all the ordinary people of Provence...

Bartoumieu.

The fishwife.

ion line. Between 240,000 and 250,000 santons are produced every year. Business is most prosperous in the Arles-Nimes-Aubagne area. *Santons* are sold only through shops. The firm exports to neighbouring countries:Switzerland, Belgium and Germany. Carbonel santons are not dressed: they are in painted baked clay. There have not always been electric kilns. The santons were "raw" and were painted by the "détrempe" (distemper) technique with a gouache mixture of gum arabic and ground pigments.

The Arlesian woman.

The same technique is still used, but the santons are baked in a kiln. There are precise stages: 1) plaster molding, 2) pressing, 3) drying, 4) scraping of joints, 5) baking, and 6) painting by hand. There are 750 sorts of santon. All production work is carried out in Marseille by local people who treasure the beauty of handicraft. Paradoxically, the santons of Provence are made in Marseille, which is not really a Provençal town. New models are created every year. Every one of them has a different attitude, size and face. There is no social segregation in the little world of the santons: the figures include the rich and poor, noblemen and beggars, young and old. Designs change with the times. They are inspired by the little trades and people of Provence. They were first created to celebrate the birth of Jesus, on the evening of December 24th. But nowadays, even atheists have a Christmas crib. Beyond the religious symbolism, the Christmas crib symbolizes a family celebration.

With devotion to his craft, grandfather Carbonel has left his grandson some maxims: enthusiasm and pleasure are essential, the santons that are inspired by the death of others are thus a hymn to life, and this quotation from the Provençal writer, Rougie: "The santon makers act the part of God the Father". ∾

The "Traditionnels" *fabrics with their* Fleur d'Arles, Petite Fleur des Champs, Petite Mouche, *and* Fleur de Maussane *patterns.*

PROVENCAL FABRICS

by Jean-Pierre Demery

Young girl wearing head-dress and shawl in Provençal fabric.

Born in Tarascon, Jean-Pierre Demery runs Souleiado, the world-famous firm of Provençal fabric makers, which was founded by his father Charles Demery in 1939.

The origins of Provençal fabrics, with their instantly recognizable, brightly-colored patterns, go back to the 17th century. When the Compagnie des Indes (Indian Trading Company) was founded, ships from the Far East and the trading posts of Sudrate and Madras brought the famous

"Foulard" *bedspread.*

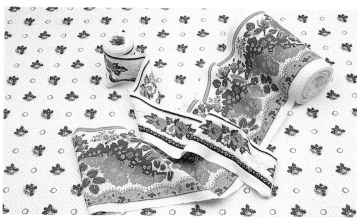

The "Pompadour" *range with its* Printemps *and* Mouriès *patterns.*

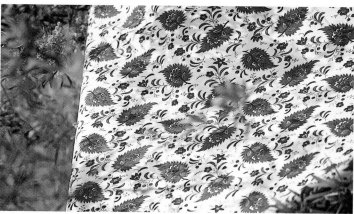

The Tramontane,
one of the "Traditionnels" range of fabrics.

Indian cotton fabrics to the port of Marseille. The aristocracy and the upper middle class were particularly fond of these painted or printed cotton textiles. Since they were rare and costly, the local craftsmen decided to start their own production in Marseille, Avignon, Nimes, Orange and other places.

They decorated these fabrics with everything that Provence inspired in them. Until 1975, printing was done by means of wooden blocks on which patterns were carved. These pattern blocks can still be admired in the Charles Demery Museum. The master dyer was an alchemist of color who worked with vegetable and mineral dyes, curcuma bulbs, oak-gall, cochineal insects, madder and sumac indigo. Nowadays, our designers still take inspiration from the 6,000 wooden blocks - the family business's veritable archives - adapting the patterns to current taste and using them on the different fabric media. The evocative little Provençal motif or pattern adorns scarves, shirts, waistcoats, skirts, dresses, ties, tablecloths, napkins and bathroom linen as well as crockery and furniture. Thus Souleiado has become the expression of a certain Provençal culture. Motifs consist of flowers, vines, herbs and olive trees; the colors are bronze, mauve and olive green. With time, the style has changed to geometric, stylized figures. Currently, the dominant trend is towards beige and Africa. So the Provençal motifs are enlarged and colored with African tones. But, whatever the trend, the design is always based on the Provençal motif, and the fabric's warmth, a faithful reflection of our land of Provence, remains intact. ⌒

Salernes tileworks.

The "tommette" traditional Provençal floor tile.

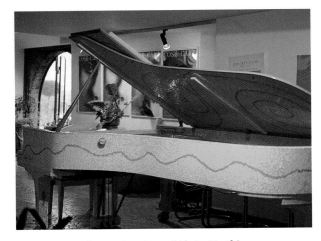

Ceramic piano (Alain Vagh).

SALERNES TILES

by
Alain Vagh

Alain Vagh, the "crazy ceramics artist", creates ceramic sets for television (e.g. "Le Cercle de Minuit") and for films (e.g. "Manon des Sources" by Claude Berry).

Salernes has everything that is needed for working clay. It is in an area of clay in a wooded region, and there is plenty of water. It has become a major ceramics centre, specializing in the production of floor and wall tiles, mainly the "tommette", a small hexagonal floor tile that was most popular between 1820 and 1914. It was revived in the 1960's with the construction of Port-Grimaud and the fashion for natural, locally-made products. Salernes has a population of 3,500 and lives from its manufacturing activity all year round. There are now twenty workshops employing a total of three hundred people. Direct selling is developing with the creation of boutiques, shops and showrooms in the village that sell everything for the home. Many of us export abroad. I set up business in Salernes in 1968. There are now shops bearing my name in New York and Berlin. I have made sets for television studios, and the tommettes for the old man's house in the film "Manon des Sources". The village has a special dynamic. It is not very big, but when you are here, you have the impression that everything is three times as big.

THE FAIENCE OF MOUSTIERS-SAINTE-MARIE

by
Alain
Ducasse

One of Moustiers's best promoters is the illutrious chef Alain Ducasse, who, in addition to managing the Alain Ducasse restaurant in Paris and the Louis XV in Monte Carlo, also runs the Bastide de Moustiers.

The lines of white houses in Moustiers stand on either side of a Romanesque bell-tower, nestling in a rocky hollow at the bottom of a breathtaking gap between impressive limestone cliffs. Hanging high in the air on a chain slung between two giant stone pillars is a star that was offered in thanksgiving by the knight de Blacas on returning from his long captivity on the Barbary Coast However, Moustiers is most famous for its faience (tin-glazed earthenware), which has been made by local craftsmen since the 17th century.

The faience crockery for which Moustiers is famous.

It reaches perfection in its "beautiful milky white glaze that plays with light and color, and its old-fashioned yet modern ornamentation". Some say the faience makers have to be a little like sorcerers to obtain such a result. Bastide de Moustiers, which once belonged to a master faience maker, has been restored and refurbished by local craftsmen. "I wanted this inn to be warm and welcoming, like this area, so that all our patrons would feel at home. My cuisine is rich in the tastes of Provence and the Mediterranean, rustic but delicate, and sometimes surprising. It highlights local produce from the Bastide's own vegetable plot and from local markets". The inn, which is near the Verdon gorges, offers a taste of Provence all year round. "I fell in love with Moustiers and its surroundings", he exclaims, "I wanted a pleasant place to spend my weekends. So I decided to create a country house for lovers of Provence and Giono". Naturally, Alain Ducasse gives pride of place to the faience of Moustiers.

His crockery, decorated by Florine Asch, is from the "Soleil" workshop, and the lounge - called the "*Salon des Faïenciers*" - is decorated with pieces by the village's various faience makers. ❦

Moustiers-Sainte-Marie sitting below the gap in the cliffs.

PERSONALITIES OF PROVENCE

Sorting the bulls.

JACQUES BON, CAMARGUE RANCHER

The Camargue rancher,
Jacques Bon.

Jacques Bon has always lived in the Camargue. Owner of "Mas de Peint", a magnificent hotel in the traditional local style, he is also a cattle rancher, sheep breeder and crop farmer.

Previous pages:
The traditional trident of the "gardian"
(Camargue cowboy).

On the "manade" (Camargue ranch).

I like the good sense of the people of the Camargue and Provence. They are level-headed people. I take pride in having managed to keep this farm and in having restored it. I like to share the Camargue with people who often come from afar. The Camargue is unique, different from the rest of Provence, a region within a region. We must look after this treasure and treat it with care. We must refuse a certain type of development in order to preserve the character of the region. The bravest and most courageous of the bulls go to the bullrings. The other 97% are for the consumer market.

A "gardian" and his horse in the Camargue.

The head "gardian" (cowboy) selects them. My herd is made up of 150 cows, 80 calves and several horses that the visitors can mount. The ranchers exchange bulls according to their characters in order to improve the breeds, for, while some are good, others are totally useless. The Cocarde Contest is a game, even if the cow's horns can cause injury. By the age of three one can tell if they are suitable for bullfighting or not, otherwise they are used for beef. We only keep the best of the herd. Unlike other ranches, we remove the young cows when we bring in the bull, in order to safeguard their development. I have spent my life managing men, and my ambition has always been to choose them on the bottom rung and watch them climb the ladder. I look for intelligence, common sense, willpower and backbone. The Camargue is a demanding place. I am dedicated to showing people its authentic side. It is a full time job. ⌇

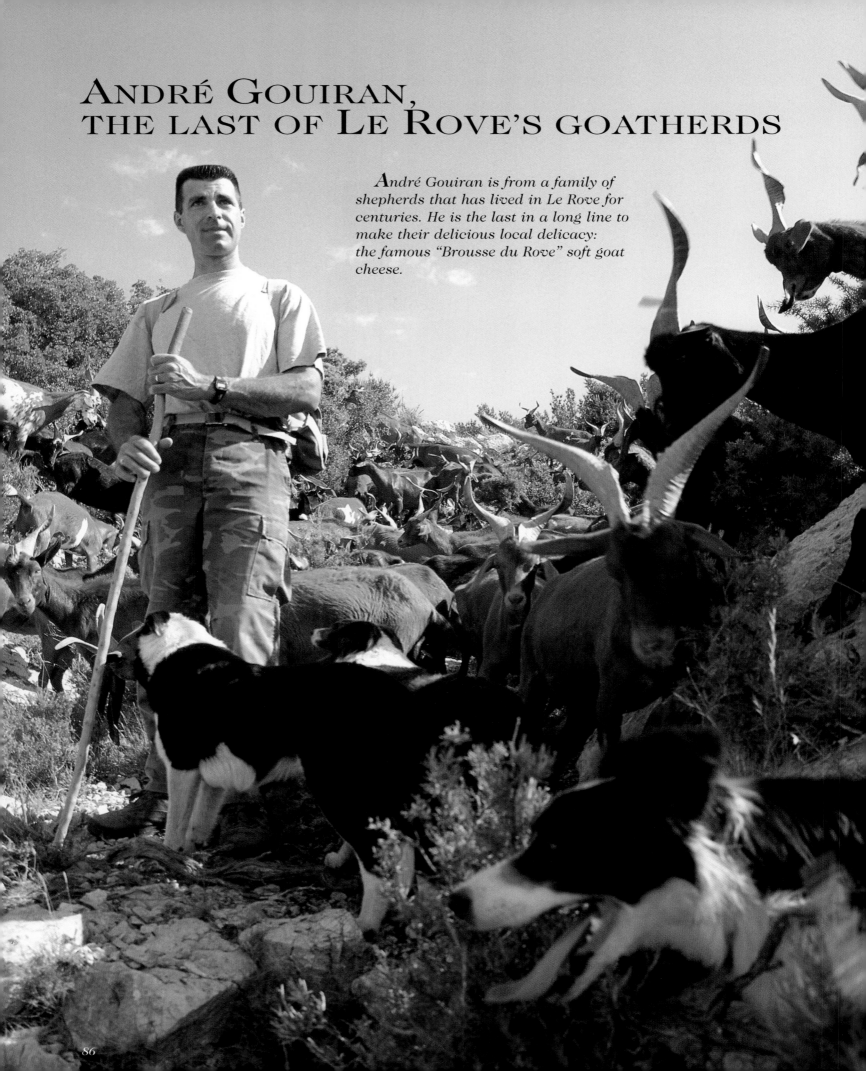

ANDRÉ GOUIRAN, THE LAST OF LE ROVE'S GOATHERDS

André Gouiran is from a family of shepherds that has lived in Le Rove for centuries. He is the last in a long line to make their delicious local delicacy: the famous "Brousse du Rove" soft goat cheese.

*Le Rove goats
with their long lyre-shaped horns.*

We raise a breed of goats with long lyre-shaped horns that is specific to Le Rove. Its origins go back to Massalia (as Marseille was known in ancient times). These hardy, very sturdy goats, have developed through natural selection: they are the only ones that can live in this arid land, with no water and very little vegetation. The people of Le Rove have been rearing goats since 1480. In 1900, there were 4,000 goats. Now there are just the 200 of my herd. I take them out onto the hillsides for four or five hours every day. My wife makes the *brousse* and the *fromageons,* and I look after the paperwork and the deliveries. We only do business with shopkeepers in the Marseille area, particularly the Marrou and Bataille delicatessens.

I am very attached to the countryside. In the hills, I follow in the footsteps of my forefathers. I sometimes find their initials engraved in stones. It is part of my soul. I especially love the hill called La Magnante, from where there is a wonderful view across the Islands of Frioul, the Château d'If, Mount Sainte Victoire, Garlaban Rock and even Mount Ventoux, on a clear day. I also love the caves - there are a lot of them around here. The most spectacular covers 200 square metres and is called the "lions' cave" because there is a rock shaped like a lion in the middle of it. I practise a traditional trade and I try to perpetuate the spirit of my ancestors, particularly in making goat cheese according to the finest traditional techniques. But I am a man of my times. I combine tradition and modernity. ∼

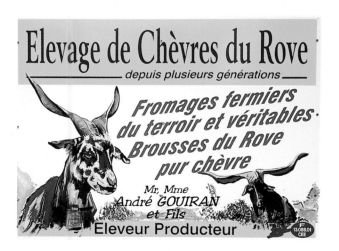

The charm of the Luberon around Ménerbes.

YVES ROUSSET-ROUARD, MAYOR OF MÉNERBES,

Writer and Film Producer

Yves Rousset-Rouard is a man who loves a challenge. He is always eagerly working on several projects at the same time. Film producer, writer, Mayor of Ménerbes, former Member of Parliament for the Vaucluse area, director of the weekly "Le Comtadin", he founded the world's only Corkscrew Museum and Domaine de la Citadelle with the same enthusiasm that drove him in 1980 when he launched the French Challenge for the Americas Cup.

MENERBES: a place of history

The name Ménerbes refers to the goddess Minerva. It has been inhabited since prehistoric times, as shown by the

*Ménerbes hill, a fortress
and a picturesque village.*

Pichouno Dolmen - one of the rare examples in the Upper Provence area - and the archaeological digs carried out on the site. The village is built on top of a rocky promontory that Nostradamus compared to a stone ship. After being under the influence of Massalia (as Marseille was known in ancient times) it developed during the Pax Romana due to the fact that it was near the Via Domitia, a major trade route between Gaul and Rome. According to tradition, the large monastery of Manacha de Saint Castor was built in Ménerbes.

A number of 9th century sarcophagi and the remains of religious buildings were recently found in Saint-Estève. The town really established its place in history during the 16th century wars of religion.

The Protestants took Ménerbes and occupied it for five years, during which the town resisted fifteen months of siege by 6,000 soldiers and artillery until Henri of Navarre negotiated the honourable evacuation of the garrison. The people of Ménerbes greatly prized their privileges and only supported the French Revolution and agreed to their integration into France with some reluctance. However, two baron generals - Robert and Carmejane - were from the town. Clovis Hugues, the first Socialist elected to the French Parliament, often mentions his native village in his writings. During the Second World War, Ménerbes was a stronghold of the French Resistance. In the last few decades, the town and its beautiful setting have attracted many famous artists including Dora Maar, Picasso, Nicolas de Staël and Georges de Pogédaïeff, who have thus helped to establish Ménerbe's reputation. ❧

The Citadel of Ménerbes.

"Petit Saint Jean" Festival in Valréas.

LITTLE SAINT JOHN, PROTECTOR OF VALRÉAS

The classical elegance of Simiane Castle's main courtyard.

Valréas: Bell-tower of the Church of Notre Dame (11th & 15th century).

The Popes' Enclave is composed of four towns: Valréas, Visan, Richerenches and Grillon. The area is an enclave in two senses: firstly, as a property of the Holy See since the 14th century, isolated within the kingdom of France; and then in 1793, a Decree of the National Convention attached it to the Vaucluse Département even though it is geographically located in the Drôme Département! This rather underlines its unique nature.

In Valréas, the capital of this singular district, is Simiane Castle, the birthplace of Pauline de Grignan, grand-daughter of Mme de Sévigné, a splendid two-storey

Simiane Castle, Valréas.

building prolonged by terraces. The Enclave Exhibition devoted to Provençal painters is held in the castle in the summer. The town also has a surprising museum of cardboard boxes. However, the major attraction is definitely the "Petit Saint Jean" - the Festival of Little Saint John, the town's protector. It takes place on the evening of 23 June, and brings us back five hundred years into the past.

This tradition steeped in history and legend goes back to 1504. At that time, the Municipality decided to no longer bring out the precious relics of Martin-des-Ulmes from the Cordeliers Monastery. To protect them, it had them replaced at the head of the procession by an effigy of Saint John the Baptist. Later, St John was represented by a child, chosen from among the boys of 3 to 5 years old whose parents have resided in Valréas for at least ten years.

Every year, at nightfall on 23 June, the whole town is in jubilation. More than 400 costumed representatives of the different neighbourhoods, trade associations and guilds take part with their banners and standards. In 1961, an Order of Companions of Saint John was even created to defend and promote this tradition. The event takes place in four stages. During the Petit Cortège (Little Procession), the previous year's Little Saint John is carried on horseback to Simiane Castle. His successor's Enthronement Ceremony takes place in the main courtyard. Then the torchlit Grand Cortège (Great Procession) moves through the packed streets. The Apothéose (Grand Finale) breaks out when the procession returns to Simiane Castle. An enchanting pageant inaugurates the one year reign of the town's child protector. ⌒

Méailles village & the "Pinewoods train" in the heart of Upper Provence.

ANDRÉ BENEDETTI AND THE "PINEWOODS TRAIN"

The jagged outline of the Cians gorge.

*T*he Societe des Chemins de Fer de Provence railway company runs a train between Nice and Digne, serving all localities on the 151 km route. It is the picturesque "Train des Pignes" or "Pinewoods Train". Andre Benedetti, a retired primary school teacher and deputy Mayor of Touet-le-Var, is one of its ardent defenders. He founded and chairs a society called "The Schoolchildren and Railways of Provence".

A train with panache.

The train travels at low speed. You have plenty of time to admire the scenery. Apart from the planned stops at stations, you can request a stop at the little shelters placed along the track. You can travel on the Pinewoods Train, but you can also stop and share the life of the local people. It is part of our collective legacy and part of the heritage of Provence.

Our society was founded in March 1998 during the Nice trade fair, to promote communication between the schoolchildren of the towns and villages served by the Chemins de Fer de Provence railway company. The railway station is a meeting-place.

The Pinewoods Train, whose first section was opened in 1891 between Digne and Mezel, carries passengers, goods and mail. People have actively campaigned to preserve it. Our aim is to make it better known and to give a voice to children, for example, by organizing competitions and various events. The train goes through two very different areas: the Maritime Alps and the Alps of Upper Provence. One is inhabited, strongly influenced by the sea, the other is much vaster, quieter and mountainous. You go from the blue sea and palm trees of the coast to the snow-topped mountains of Valberg and the archaeological riches of Digne.

Cians gorges:
the end of the world.

Landscape of upper Provence: Lure Mountain.

GIONO'S PROVENCE

by René Frégni

Manosque: Mont d'Or.

Let me tell you how I first entered the world of Jean Giono. For twenty years, he has never ceased to move me. Every day I open one of his novels and savor a few pages to experience that intense yet simple pleasure of embarking on a journey, or watching the spectacle of a woman crossing her silk-clad legs as she sits outside a café, or relishing a vanilla ice cream on a June evening in a quiet area of Venice.

I discovered Giono late in life, while walking. For ten months, I had been walking to warm up my bones in a freezing military prison. It was in Verdun, and I was nineteen years old. One day my cell door opened and the chaplain said: "Here, read that, it's by someone from Provence, like yourself". The door closed and my teeth were still chattering. I looked at the cover of the little blue book called "Colline" and saw a herd of goats coming towards me. I sat on the sloping bench that served as a bed and opened the book.

Bones in a freezing military prison. It was in Verdun, and I was nineteen years old. One day my cell door opened and the chaplain said: "Here, read that, it's by someone from Provence, like yourself". The door closed and my teeth were still chattering. I looked at the cover of the little blue book called "Colline" and saw a herd of goats coming towards me. I sat on the sloping bench that served as a bed and opened the book.

I was spellbound. After a few words, my cell was flooded with the whole of my childhood: the sun-scorched village of Saint-Maime on its rocky outcrop overgrown with thyme, the smell of hens, a swirling fountain, the cosy sound of the pigeons on the roof in the morning, or the golden pearl of sunlight that comes in through a hole in the shutter and rolls slowly across the front of a chest of drawers, then suddenly lights up the whole bedroom when it strikes the brass bedstead.

The River Durance: Chapel of Saint Madeleine under Mirabeau Bridge.

Suddenly a magical sun was shining on me, chasing away the cold. When I arrived in Manosque a few months later, Giono had just died. One evening in November 1970 I went to the cemetery to see this man who had left me this lifelong gift of a shining sun that glows in my mind.

From then on, I was slowly drawn into a world of dreams. I rode with Angelo, the little hussar, and I slipped through narrow rooflights into fantastical lofts, and then I started to dream of Pauline every night. I went down into a grand house with marble stairs and saw a young woman holding a candelabra to her little pointed face. For five years, I was madly in love with her, and I thought I caught a glimpse of her one

General view of Manosque.

hundred times in the narrow streets of Manosque. So where was this loft of my dreams? I had only one clue: there were 23 steps between each floor and the next. Everywhere I went, I got into the habit of counting the steps. One afternoon, as I went up the stairs of the library in the Herbès Mansion, I counted 23 steps. I ran back down and counted them again: there really were 23 steps! My heart skipped a beat.

After that, I sat for whole afternoons in one of the library rooms, pretending to read a book. I knew I would meet a woman of great beauty and courage. One evening, she entered. I recognised her. Since then,

we meet every evening somewhere in the town and we go to look for Angelo. We leave our car in the village of Le Contadour and walk through a meagre valley of lavender, loose stones and rye to Pas-de-Redortiers, where it all began. Perhaps you think I'm making this all up? Well, think again! One thing Jean Giono taught me is that stories are the only true things in life. If you want to meet Pauline, follow my example: leave your daily routine behind and go up onto the rooftops - do not look any further, for happiness awaits you there.

You must go blindfold into the kingdom of the hills and set free your inner self. For mystery is the science of the poet. ∽

The village of Lorgues.

BRUNO, AN IMPASSIONED ENTHUSIAST

Bruno, chef and restaurant owner in Lorgues, showing a giant truffle.

With his exuberant gestures and his booming voice, Bruno is bursting with talent and vitality. Lordly, easy-going, warm-hearted and humorous, he has a real sense of friendly hospitality. People come to his place from all over the world. His patrons are loyal; many become his friends. Born by chance in Toulon, he identifies with Lorgues, his true homeland. Standing in front of his stoves, Bruno is a happy man: he lives out his passion for the truffle.

Lorgues: Elegant country house.

"*Chez Bruno*" was originally the house of Mariette, my grandmother. She brought me up. She gave me my taste for cooking. My grandparents earned this house with the sweat of their brows. I am very attached to it. I settled here out of loyalty to my grandmother and re-arranged it to pursue my life's passion. I opened in 1983 with the truffle as my vocation. I use 3,000 kg of truffles every year. I grew up under a truffle oak! I wanted to share my pleasures with others, starting very simply by serving table d'hote dinners. Now, people come from all over the world to taste fine dishes at "Chez Bruno".

When you give people pleasure, they appreciate it and do not forget. I was lucky to be born in the Var area. I love this region - its sun, light, olive trees and pines. With its geographical situation and its mountains, the Var area is both rich and poor: on the one hand, there is Saint Tropez; on the other, a remote farmhouse without electricity. The centre of the Departement is a vast empty space, almost deserted. At the same time, it is a wonderful reservoir for the future. The price of land is still reasonable. There is beautiful scenery and an enormous expanse of forest. The Var area boasts the oldest vineyards in Europe, and they are now rapidly expanding.

The quality of Var wines has improved enormously: they can hold their own with the best of them. The whole upland area supplies truffles - white in summer, black in winter - and morels and other mushrooms in all seasons. The local fresh produce is wonderful. So we have to be careful to preserve our roots and this outstanding quality of life. One visits the Var like a monument, a cathedral of greenery.

JIMMY GIBBEZ, PAINTER, AND LE VIEUX CANNET

The American painter Jimmy Gibbez left New York in 1960 to travel around the world. He has exhibited his paintings in Paris, Amsterdam, England and Switzerland. He settled in France a long time ago, and now lives in Le Vieux Cannet des Maures, a little village in the middle of the Var region. And when people ask where he comes from, he says: "Le Vieux-Cannet".

Interior of Jimmy Gibbez's house.

After studying music and art in the United States, I was bitten by the travel bug. I left for Europe and I have stayed here. I worked in haute couture and show business, and did society portraits and interior decoration. Now I live in Le Vieux Cannet des Maures, the centre of my world. I have gone from the infinitely large to the infinitely small. This village of forty people located on a rocky spur, a stone's throw from St-Tropez, has not changed for 2,000 years. Time passes it by. It is a hamlet with

Le Vieux Cannet village square.

the soul of a village and a great history. It is peaceful in both winter and summer. Every time I go in through the old stone porch at the entrance to the village, I feel at home. Like in all Provençal villages, the cats rule. By a piece of good fortune, ever since I was given the job of doing the Christmas shop windows of the famous Hermès shops in 1987 for their 150th anniversary - in which I depicted cats dressed up in 18th century finery - cats have become my companions in life and work. Officially, I have five cats in the house. Their many feline friends come to visit me and watch me painting in my studio in a 12th century monastery. ✍

As if carried by the foliage: Le Vieux Cannet, where Jimmy Gibbez lives.

The island of Les Embiez.

PAUL RICARD

by
Patricia Thoulouze,
Paul Ricard's
granddaughter

Looking for the "Pataclé" secret recipe.

With his friend Fernandel.

Of all the famous figures of Provence, it is he whose name is pronounced millions of times every day. His exciting life has made a legend of him. The name Paul Ricard evokes the very essence of Provence.

He grew up in Marseille, experiencing the joys and pains of ordinary people at the start of the century. His grandfather, a baker, gave him his love of work, local heritage and tradition. With his father, a wine merchant, he travelled all over Provence with a horse and cart, from the Camargue to Le Castellet, via La Gineste, the *calanques*, Marseille's Old Harbor and L'Estaque. According to legend, it was an old man from the hills of Aubagne, "old man Espanet", who gave the young Paul the secret of his *"pataclé"*, a mixture of aromatic plants and essences that was to become the Ricard anise drink. He remained very attached to the living, magnificent Provence and its warm, colorful people, and he spent his whole life promoting it.

In the 1930's, the young Paul charmed everyone with his *pastis*. With promotional verve, he revived forgotten feasts and festivals, such as the Tarasque of Tarascon, going from fair to banquet in village after village. Together with his friends Pagnol, Fernandel, Tino Rossi and Vincent Scotto, he revealed Provence to a France that was astonished to discover its southern dimension. Europe discovered the warmth and *joie de vivre* of Provence in this disconcerting combination of cold water and Ricard. Lastly, Paul Ricard devoted himself to his other love: the two "sunshine islands", just off the Var coast. He built a theater, artists' studios and crafts shops on the island of Bendor, bringing it back to life. Paul Ricard loved the crystal-watered creeks of Les Embiez island, its cliffs facing the open sea, its gently sloping vineyards and its trees free to bend in the wind. On these two heavenly islands, he never ceased to glorify the Provence of his childhood, with its values and its colors Like a grateful child, Provence returned the favor, making Ricard one of its essential symbols. ❧

The Paul Ricard legend.

Jean Franval at Daudet's Windmill.

Jean Franval, journey of a Provencal actor

A man of the theater, director of the company that bears his name, Jean Franval lives in Tarascon, where he was born. His roots are Provençal. For five years, he has also owned a house in Les Saintes Maries de la Mer.

35 years later, the return home to the Camargue.

First of all I ran a bar in Sambuc, in the middle of the Camargue. I sang, told stories, and had guest artists. Then I took over a café-restaurant in Mas Thibert. I started my singing and music-hall career after this experience. Then I auditioned for the Marseille Opera. But I wasn't made for opera and I didn't have any musical training. My stage name comes from Franceschi, my real name, of Corsican origin. I know the Camargue well. I harvested rice. I cleaned out field drains. We were in the water up to our bellies and we couldn't work more than four hours a day. Then, on impulse, I went up to Paris, where I knew nobody. I auditioned and worked in cabarets. One day as I was coming out of the Olympia, I met the comedian Fernand Reynaud, whom I had met in a cabaret in Lyon. I did sketches with him for five years. Some people recognized the real comedian in me. I started with Jean Carmé in "Douze hommes en colère". I got the theater bug. I played all the roles that required a real southern accent.

Then Jacques Ertaud got me to play Vitays in "Rémi sans famille", the first French TV series bought by the Americans. I stayed thirty-five years in Paris from 1954 to 1989., then I came back to Provence to live. With the help of grants from the Regional Council, I managed to put together my own troupe, "La Compagnie Théâtrale Jean Franval". I acted in "La femme du boulanger". Pagnol's stories are universal. I have been perform-ing Pagnol for nine years. Once he told me I was made for the great roles. Unfortunately he died before he could write one for me!

ARTS AND FESTIVALS
OF PROVENCE

Performance of "Curlew River" by Benjamin Britten.

AIX-EN-PROVENCE OPERA FESTIVAL

by Hélène Lublin

*The forum of Place des Cardeurs,
a friendly gathering-place.*

*Previous pages:
Performance of "Turandot" in the
Roman Theater, Orange.*

Aix-en-Provence:
The sparkling Rotonde fountain.

Aix-en-Provence is the city of music, with its International Opera Festival, which recently celebrated its 50th anniversary. Founded in 1948 by Gabriel Dussurget, it is famous for the quality of its repertoire (mainly devoted to Mozart), the talent of its invited artists (including Teresa Stich-Randall, Teresa Berganza, Luigi Alva and Rolando Panerai) and the wonderful setting in which it is held: the splendid Archevêché Theater, which is now indissociable from the Festival. Great conductors such as Hans Rosbaud and Carlo Maria Guilini have taken part in the Festival and, in its early days, great contemporary figures such as Cassandre, Masson, Derain and Balthus were also involved. When Bernard Lefort became director in 1974, the repertoire expanded to include bel canto, as it did when his successor, Louis Erlo, introduced the baroque repertoire.

I have been in three productions in the Aix Festival. The first time, I was eighteen years old. It was in 1968, and I had extraordinary luck. I was just a beginner, and I came to replace a singer three months before the first performance. I was auditioned by Gabriel Dussurget, who often gave young female singers their first break. At the time, the Festival had a very intimate atmosphere, which gradually disappeared as it became more successful. It is now an essential part of the opera calendar and an international event. I love the south of France: Aix, but also Marseille.

Mount Sainte Victoire from Combe de Bimont - *Justinien Gaut (1817-1880) - Musée Granet, Aix-en-Provence.*

SAINTE-VICTOIRE AND THE PAINTERS

The massive hulk of Mount Sainte Victoire:
a mythical mountain
that has inspired painters and poets.

The Aix countryside has been compared to a great Greco-Latin garden dwarfed by a revered mountain: Mount Sainte Victoire, which reaches a height of over 1,000 metres. "Temple and altar, spirit and rock", wrote Joseph d'Arbaud, "its presence casts a spell over the landscape".

The mountain bears all the strata of history: dinosaur bones were discovered at its foot, its name comes from the ancient victory of Marius over the Barbarians, and the centuries have each left their mark on its slopes and surroundings. This explains its fascination for artists. Paul Constant compares Sainte Victoire to Moby Dick: through it, everyone confronts their own white whale. Monster and protecting divinity, focal point of life and landmark, it

Mount Sainte Victoire from a farmyard - *François Marius-Granet (1775-1849)*
Musée Granet, Aix-en-Provence.

defines and illuminates the landscape. It seized Jean Giono's imagination. "The mountain", he said, "with its fantastic sails of white rocks, is like a phantom ship in the light of day". He stresses its artistic interest.

Many painters of all styles have been inspired by Sainte Victoire: François-Marius Granet, after whom a museum in Aix is named, and who is sometimes considered the least Provençal of the painters of Provence, painted some freely spirited watercolors of the mountain. The subject has been explored by Jean Antoine Constantine, a pioneer of painting "from nature"; Prosper Grécy, who was fond of rocky landscapes; Marius Espalière, Justinien Gaut, Emile Loubon (whose dynamic style brings the mass of rock to life), Barthélémy Niollon, Philippe Soleri and Joseph Ravaisou, who are generally considered part of the school of the Provençal masters.

However, it is unquestionably Cézanne's genius that towers over this mountain, which he examined from all angles and which he made his own, to the extent that one cannot mention Sainte Victoire without thinking of Cézanne. Sainte Victoire was painted by Renoir, and in more recent times, by André Masson and Pierre tal-Coat, Yves Brayer and today's shining examples of the Provençal school, such as Yvette Bonté, Georges Briata and Jean-Claude Quilici. ⌒

Mount Sainte Victoire from Chemin des Lauves
Paul Cézanne (1839-1906)
Musée Granet, Aix-en-Provence.

The Roman Amphitheatre in Arles, where beautiful and deadly rites are perpetuated.

Arles, town of Bull-fighting and the Arts

by Yvan Audouard

Yvan Audouard, one of Provence's greatest writers, with the publisher Marc Crès.

Yvan Audouard is one of Provence's most eminent figures. Author of more than eighty books, twenty films, three plays, hundreds of radio and television programmes, and famous satirical chronicles in the "Canard Enchaîné", this tireless storyteller personifies a form of humor and a culture that are special to Provence.

"**I** am pleased with this year's feria - the bullfighting festival. Until the last day, there were almost no bulls, but there was plenty of sun. This is rare because the Arles feria, the first of the year, is held at Easter, when the weather is not always good.

Bullfighter in dazzling costume.

Arles: Place de la République, at the crossroads of the centuries.

And for me, the feria is a tragedy in the sun. It was once an equestrian show given by very talented horsemen. The history of bullfighting is simple: the noblemen rode on horseback and their valets helped them. Then the latter turned the unmounted bullfight into a true spectacle. Nowadays, it is no longer the noblemen who ride on horseback, but their valets.

A great love affair is not one that ends badly, but one that ends so well that we forget how it started so badly. That is what the feria means to me. Arles is the town of my teenage years, the first encounters with the fair sex, and the first emotions. It was also there that I studied the Humanities. It is easier to study Greek tragedy in Arles than anywhere else: sitting in the Roman Theater brings one closer to the classical writers and brings

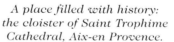

A place filled with history: the cloister of Saint Trophime Cathedral, Aix-en Provence.

learning alive. As you walk through the narrow streets of Arles, look upwards, and you will see insignia, statues of the Virgin Mary, and columns. History is everywhere. In Zurich, you walk on ten storeys of strongrooms and gold ingots, but in Arles, you walk on 2,000 years of history and tens of thousands of years of prehistory. It is a town with a feeling of timelessness where it is easy to imagine the past. Arles is continually being revived. I love everything about this town, where I always discover something different.

There is the famous International Photography Festival where I was moved by the photographs, both industrial and non-commercial. Arles is a town where photographers can lie while telling the truth. They help you to bring out the poetry that is in you and in the hearts of everyone.

(From an interview) .

The Ariane Mnouchkine Theatre Company.

AVIGNON THEATER FESTIVAL

by Jean Boissieu

For fifty-three years, the whole town of Avignon has been invaded and virtually possessed by the theater every summer, from July 10th to the end of the month or longer. However, apart from the name and the dates, is there anything in common between the Festival founded by Jean Vilar in 1947 and that of today? Originally, faced with the crisis of the entertainment business in the years after the Second World War, the Festival was the initiative of a man convinced of the formative role and the vital importance of the theater. He spoke of "popular theater" and "theater as a public service". A permanent company - known as the Théâtre National Populaire - was formed around him from 1951 to 1966.

Famous actors and future stars including Gérard Philippe, Maria Casarès, Germaine Montero, Jeanne Moreau and Philippe Noiret joined the company in all humility. There was only one indoor theater - in the Popes' Palace - plus two open-air venues. The repertoire was largely classical, mainly composed of Corneille, Molière and Shakespeare, but it also included previously banned German works by romantics such as Kleist and contemporary playwrights such as Brecht. Without scenery, the austere productions appeared revolutionary, while their technique was purely classical. The great innovation was no doubt in its form of organization, the virtually permanent contact with the public, and the reasonably-priced inclusive packages for accommodation and theater tickets.

From 1966, Jean Vilar, who had resigned as director of the TNP, invented the "second Avignon festival" - called the "Off" (the festival "fringe"). It took into account the cultural transformation that had

Avignon: The famous "Pont d'Avignon", with the Popes' Palace in the background.

An international event: Avignon Theater Festival.

preceded it and whose effects, in parallel with the upheaval of 1968, continued under the direction of Paul Parax after Vilar's death in May 1971. Since then, Avignon really has been "taken over by the theater" and by all forms of the creative arts - dance, musical drama, film and the plastic arts - with all possible venues, including cloisters, occupied by the arrival in force of the fringe festival. Even if we do not count the fringe events (which are difficult to quantify) or Avignon's permanent companies such as Le Chêne Noir, Les Halles, Le Balcon and Le Bélier - which all could be said to organize their own little festivals within the great festival - there are sometimes more than two hundred productions in around twenty different venues in certain years.

With very different artistic approaches but the same intellectual integrity, Vilar's successors - Alain Crombecque and now Bernard Faivre d'Arcier - will not be able to prevent the development of a third Avignon festival, that of the present consumer society. In today's crowd, professionals scouting for talent rub shoulders with hungry theater-goers who try desperately to see a record number of events, rushing from theater to theater and from one seat (or bench) to another, from eleven o'clock in the morning until midnight. Nevertheless, there is still enough of the original spirit left for the Avignon summer experience to provide some surprises and great pleasure.

The back wall of the Roman Theater's stage. Set of the opera "Turandot".

THE CHOREGIES D'ORANGE FESTIVAL

Orange: Detail of the back wall of the Roman Theater's stage.

by Raymond Duffaut, director of Chorégies d'Orange since 1980

Orange: General view of the Roman Theater from the tiered seats.

The Chorégies d'Orange festival was founded in 1869 by Antony Réal and Félix Ribert, two members of the Félibre Provençal cultural revival movement. Ever since it first started with an opera by Joseph Méhul, the festival has continued to bring together different kinds of productions (music, drama and opera). Held in the magnificent setting of Orange's Roman Theatre, which is on UNESCO's world heritage list, the "Roman Festival" that preceded the present Chorégies d'Orange festival mainly presented drama and Greco-Latin productions directed by Frédéric Mistral. After 1947, the Chorégies, which was then the summer residence of the Comédie Française, declined under competition from the Avignon Theatre Festival founded by Jean Vilar. In 1971, on the initiative of Jacques Bourgeois, it again moved into the limelight by concentrating exclusively on opera, and thus became the world-famous festival as we now know it. It has featured many great artists, including Pavarotti, Domingo, Montserrat Cabaillé, Barbara Hendricks and John Vickert. Two major new productions were created specially for the 1999 Chorégies festival: Verdi's "La Traviata" and Bellini's "Norma", which was a historic triumph twenty-five years ago. The festival venue is appreciated for the outstanding quality of its acoustics. The Roman Theatre seats 8,500 and has a stage eighty metres wide. It is the largest open air theatrical venue and is one of the few Roman theatres that has kept the back wall of its stage - which is so vital for the productions. Every member of the audience can feel the expressive subtleties of the music. Despite the great size of the Roman Theatre, the audience sit close to the stage, allowing close contact between them, the artists and the musicians. The Chorégies festival has a very large seating capacity and attracts a very broad range of people, making it a major popular festival of the highest quality. ✍

The venerable plane trees in the grounds of Florans Castle.

ROQUE D'ANTHERON PIANO FESTIVAL

by Hélène Grimaud

The young pianist Hélène Grimaud is already famous. She was born in Aix-en-Provence and now lives in the USA. The Roque d'Antheron Festival was the starting point of her career.

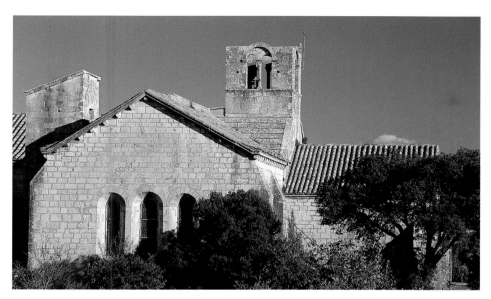

*Some of the festival's concerts
are held in Silvacane Abbey.*

The Roque d'Anthéron International Piano Festival has been going for nineteen years. It has established itself as the ren-dez-vous of the world's top performers. The Festival is held in the grounds of Florans Castle - in a setting of giant red-woods and centuries-old plane trees (365 of them: one for each day of the year) - and in other prestigious venues such as the Cistercian Silvacane Abbey or the church of Saint Louis. Music lovers rightly consider La Roque d'Antheron as the *"Mecca of the Piano"*. My first professional engagement was in La Roque d'Antheron. It was an overwhelm-ing experience. I have returned seve-ral times since then. I make an exception and travel from the USA for this festival because of my first experience, and also because of its special charm. One gets carried away with the atmosphere that lends itself to expression, and by the quasi-religious attention of the audience, who are all connoisseurs. Not only is there a beautiful setting, but there is a wonderful spirit in this magical place.

The team built around René Martin and Paul Onoratini is very energetic. The organizers allow you a lot of freedom, and they are very attentive and affectionate. For me, Provence means radiant light and colors: it is Cézanne. When I visit a museum that has some of his paintings, I always start and end with them. I am always very proud of Aix, where I was born. ∿

*The International Piano Festival and
its audience of music lovers.*

Saint Tropez: Legendary port of the Var coast (general view).

SAINT TROPEZ, A FEAST FOR THE SENSES

by Gérald Hardy

A colorful event in Saint Tropez: the "bravade".

Gérald Hardy has lived since 1991 in Saint Tropez, where he manages the select La Messardière chateau hotel.

Sénéquier café, a meeting-place of celebrities.

"*A singular wind guided me to the 8th wonder of the world*", wrote the painter Paul Lignac. It is probably the same singular wind that brings us to savour the charms of St Tropez, to cherish the area's distinctive radiance that enhances the little fishermen's houses, the vineyards on the sunlit hills, and the sparkling Mediterranean.

This unique place is double-sided, both Goddess and Starlet: a town glittering with summer sequins and stars, and a village steeped in the colors and fragrance of Provence: an astonishing symbiosis. There is the flashy, superficial St Tropez popularized through the media, but you just have take a stroll through the old narrow streets or on the harbor in the early morning to discover the soul of an older village that has survived intact under the fashionable veneer, in spite of the passage of time and changing fashions.

The air is a most tender blue with the subtlest pink hue. After a stormy night, the sunrise is exquisite over the fishing harbor or at La Ponche, where the jetty almost blends into the red rocks, maintaining its natural, untamed appearance.

In a halo of blue light, the proud and impregnable citadel towers above the red tiled roofs that are gathered around the bell-tower in tight rows stretching languidly along the harbor and around the bay, the reflection of their pink-tinged ochre facades shimmering on the water. St Tropez changes its attire and color in harmony with the seasons. The Indian Summer with its crystal-clear light lasts into November and December. The beauty of the mimosa in January and February is followed closely by the white glow of the almond blossoms. After the whims and April showers of springtime come glorious summer with its

The ochre and azure magic of the French Riviera.

swirling social life, the peace of autumn and the magnificent reddish yellows after the wine harvest. The sea, in deep blue to pearly tones, is ever-present and unchanging to our eyes.

In winter the beaches are different but still beautiful. One can enjoy a pleasant stroll and contemplate the snow-capped Alps set off against the deep green of the umbrella pines in the foreground and the vibrant red of the Esterel Mountains in the background. There is no doubt, St Tropez is a "happening" and a constant source of delight.

In winter, one will always find the real St Tropez. The beautiful setting, the climate and the art of living are simple luxuries in their own right. They are accessible to all and cannot be bought or sold: they have that priceless quality of life. "Luxury is not

The permanent exhibition by local painters
along the harbor.

Saint Tropez at night.

the opposite of poverty, but of vulgarity", Coco Chanel used to say. Does true happiness not lie in the simplest of things? If this is the case, then the pleasure and the joy of living in St Tropez, in the heart of Provence, far from the concrete cities offer, without doubt, the real luxury of happiness!

St Tropez remains the village it was, used to be, and is, for the joy of discovering it or rediscovering it from the famous bend known as "Merci Mon Dieu" (Thanks be to God). Indeed, from this bend, the view of the village remains unchanged and eternal.

From "Bravades" to "Nioulargues", many yachtsmen have met in this little port. Some have dreamed of it, all have admired it, but none have ever forgotten it. ∿

ACKNOWLEDGEMENTS

Special thanks to:

Christine Alombert

Marie Badel-Nay

Hervé Bodez

Guillaume Bourgat

Barbara & Beverly Brackett

Colette Brivet

Jacqueline Brotte

Christian Carrère

Liliane Conil

Catherine Crès-Lavalette

Jean-Michel Dasque

Georges Descrières

Anthony Di Pietro

Florence
(of Roque d'Anthéron Piano Festival)

Alexandre Gad

Anne-Marie Galvez

Laurent Genre

Géraldine
(Souleïado boutique, Marseille)

Yvon Kergal

Stéphanie Lebeau

Alain Léonard

Patrick Micel

Michel Morosoff

Max Pellegrin

Sophie Rigaud

Catherine Rollin

Nicole Sabater

Avignon Theatre Festival

Manosque Tourist Information Office

Fontaine-de-Vaucluse Tourist Information Office

Mayor & staff of Banon Town Council

Mayor & staff of Sisteron Town Council